More praise for *Live It Up without Outliving Your Money*

"It's a whole new ball game: the traditional defined-benefit corporate pension, which for decades assured the average retiree of comfortable existence, is a thing of the past. Almost as an afterthought, employers are tossing workers into self-directed defined-contribution plans and forcing them into becoming their own investment managers. With *Live It Up without Outliving Your Money*, Paul Merriman has thrown struggling employees and retired folks a lifeline—an easy-to-understand survey of the investment world and blueprint for successful portfolio management. Pick it up, read it, and secure your financial future."

—William Bernstein, author, *The Birth of Plenty* and *The Four Pillars of Investing*

"Paul's insights and process to implement a financial plan to help enable our life's dreams is inspiring! He brings starry-eyed investors back to earth and teaches them how to take-off again—more safely—with an exciting financial independence flight plan. Thank you, Paul!"

—Alan Mulally, president and CEO, Boeing Commercial Airplanes Group

"Paul's wonderful book will educate you, stimulate you, and motivate you to develop the appropriate retirement plan for your personal situation. It provides both the diagnosis and prescription."

—Larry Swedroe, director of research, Buckingham Asset Management and author, *The Only Guide to a Winning Investment Strategy You'll Ever Need*

"One of the easiest to understand explanations and illustrations showing the importance of allocation diversification I have ever read."

—Bud Hebeler, www.analyzenow.com, and author, *J.K. Lasser's Your Winning Retirement Plan*

"Paul Merriman is a practical idealist whose advice should be heeded."

—Sheldon Jacobs, editor, *The No-Load Fund Investor*

"Sage advice from a Master. Merriman pulls it all together: Investment Theory, Portfolio Strategy, Investor Psychology, and a practitioner's common sense approach to solving the great retirement riddle. There is no better road map for anyone that would like to retire in style, with financial security and peace of mind. Merriman, is your experienced and friendly guide with intimate knowledge of the terrain. He navigates his familiar retirement landscape and avoids the pitfalls with the sure confidence of a veteran who has been there done that with hundreds of personal clients."

—Frank Armstrong, president of Investor Solutions, Inc.
and author, *The Informed Investor*

"Typically, it's either or! Either you live it up during retirement and outlive your money, or you deprive yourself during retirement so that you don't outlive your money. Well, Paul Merriman provides practical and easy-to-implement advice that will let help you do both—enjoy retirement without fear of running out of money."

—Robert Powell, editor, *Retirement Weekly*—
a service of MarketWatch

"I recommend *Live It Up without Outliving Your Money!* to you . . . and your parents . . . and your children . . . and anyone else whose future you care about."

—Joseph L. Shaefer, chairman, The Stanford Advisory Group

"The most important financial decisions in your life happen *after* you retire. Paul's book is a step-by-step guide to living like a king in retirement."

—Tony Sagami, editor, Weiss Publications and president,
Harvest Advisors

"*Live It Up without Outliving Your Money* should be required reading for everyone."

—Ed Fulbright, CPA, and host of *Mastering Your Money* radio show in Durham, NC

Live It Up without Outliving Your Money!

Live It Up without Outliving Your Money!

10 Steps to a Perfect Retirement Portfolio

Paul Merriman

WILEY

John Wiley & Sons, Inc.

Published by John Wiley & Sons, Inc., Hoboken, New Jersey.
Published simultaneously in Canada.

For general information about our other products and services, please contact our Customer Care Department within the United States at 800-762-2974, outside the United States at 317-572-3993 or fax 317-572-4002.

Wiley also publishes its books in a variety of electronic formats. Some content that appears in print may not be available in electronic books. For more information about Wiley products, visit our web site at www.wiley.com.

Library of Congress Cataloging-in-Publication Data:

Merriman, Paul A., 1943–
    Live it up without outliving your money! : 10 steps to a perfect
retirement portfolio / by Paul Merriman.
        p. cm.
    Includes index.
    ISBN-13 978-0-471-67997-4 (cloth)
    ISBN-10 0-471-67997-6 (cloth)
    1. Finance, Personal.   2. Investments.   3. Financial security.
    4. Retirement income—Planning.   I. Title
    HG179.M432   2005
    332.024'014—dc22   2004027962

Printed in the United States of America

10 9 8 7 6 5 4 3

To five people who light up my life every day: my wife, Suzanne; my son, Jeff; and my three delightful daughters: Julie, Larisa, and Alexa

Acknowledgments

No duty is more urgent than giving thanks.

—St. Ambrose

I could not have written this book—and I could not do the teaching I do—without the help of many people who have generously given their time, talent, wisdom, and encouragement.

I have the good fortune to have wonderful close working partnerships with three very talented people. Tom Cock Jr. helps me reach hundreds of thousands of readers and listeners. He is my co-host on "Sound Investing," our weekly radio show, and creator of *SoundInvesting.com,* where those broadcasts are available online. Tom, who is host of the weekly PBS series "Serious Money," also makes sure that the workshops I lead are filled and oversees *FundAdvice.com,* my company's educational web site.

I could write a whole chapter on the many ways my life is enriched by my son, Jeff Merriman-Cohen. Jeff is managing partner of our company, freeing me to concentrate on what I do best. Jeff is a superb financial advisor, an excellent manager, and a pleasure to work with in every way. Perhaps best of all (and very rare), my son is a full partner and a true friend. Every father should be so lucky!

Every part of this book reflects the writing skills of Rich Buck, managing editor of *FundAdvice.com.* Rich spent 20 years as a *Seattle Times* business reporter, and all that experience shows. Rich and I have great fun together generating and developing articles. He transforms my ideas into interesting, easy reading that has helped thousands of investors since 1993.

Over the years, many people have helped me get my message out to investors. I am indebted to Craig Tolliver, who invited me to write a weekly column at *CBSMarketWatch.com*; to Ken and Daria Dolan, who invited me to be a guest on their nationally syndicated radio and television shows; to Paul Kangas of "Nightly Business Report," Humberto Cruz, a syndicated newspaper columnist, and Paul Farrell, a writer at CBSMarketWatch who shares my commitment to helping investors distinguish between what I call "investment pornography" and legitimate advice.

Bill Donoghue introduced me to thousands of investors at his Donoghue Mutual Fund Superstars conferences; Kim and Charles Githler of Intershow did the same with their wonderful Money Shows across the country. Wayne Baxmann of the American Association of Individual Investors has made it possible for me to speak at dozens of AAII chapters.

From Dan Wheeler, Bo Cornell, Eugene Fama, and Kenneth French I have learned the power of putting together world-class investments using the best mutual funds on the planet. Every reader who follows my advice in Chapters 6 through 10 is also indebted to these individuals.

Finally, I must mention two very special people in my life: Thaddeus Spratlen and Dr. Lynn Staheli. They have inspired me to realize that I don't ever want to retire, because I'm simply having too much fun and there's too much still to be done.

Thaddeus, professor emeritus at the University of Washington, was one of my teachers long ago and has been a friend for 40 years. He spent decades as a professor preparing students for successful careers. He's devoting his "retirement" years to the Business and Economic Development Program through which the University of Washington Business School and Seattle Rotary put students and experienced business professionals together to help small businesses in Seattle's inner city.

Lynn, a retired physician from Children's Hospital in Seattle, started Global-HELP (*global-help.org*), a nonpolitical, humanitarian agency that distributes free publications to medical professionals in developing countries. I'm proud to be a founding member of this organization's board.

My highest aspiration is to be like Thaddeus and Lynn.

Contents

Why I Wrote This Book

I am not a teacher but an awakener.

—Robert Frost

This book is designed in part to help investors protect themselves from Wall Street practices that I saw first-hand many years ago. Fresh out of college in the 1960s, I became a broker for a large Wall Street firm. Training classes in New York quickly taught me the priorities that should dominate my working day.

I guess I was naïve and too idealistic for Wall Street. I had looked forward to helping people with their money. It didn't take long to learn that Wall Street had only one high-priority objective: sell.

Sales, of course, required trading activity. Gradually, I realized Wall Street was infected with an attitude that didn't seem right to me: If the clients were content, they weren't doing the firm any good. No matter what the clients had done, it was the broker's job to persuade them to do something else.

Ideally, that "something else" involved buying proprietary products on which the big brokerage houses earned unusually high commissions. Sometimes brokers were offered incentives such as free trips. In most cases, the commissions and the cost of the trips were built into the price of the products. This allowed brokers to tell clients they could buy these products without paying any commission. The clients thought they were getting a special deal. We knew otherwise: They were being exploited.

I'll admit the sophisticated world of New York City held quite an allure to a young man from Wenatchee, Washington. Wall Street made the job fun, and it seemed as if there was lots of money to be made easily.

But it didn't take me long to grow weary of a job that, I realized, was designed essentially to separate people from their money with little thought given to whether these people were getting something valuable in return.

Before long, I left the brokerage industry to follow other business pursuits that brought me much more satisfaction. This eventually also gave me a level of financial success that let me open my own investment business and begin managing money for individuals in 1983. I vowed at the time to keep my business free from all conflicts of interest, and independence has allowed me to fulfill that pledge.

In working with thousands of investors since then, I have seen the unfortunate results of what happens when people do what Wall Street tells them to do.

- Millions of people who wouldn't leave on a vacation without a road map nevertheless set aside hundreds of thousands of dollars for retirement without knowing their destination or having any plan to get there.

- Investors leave the bulk of their money in popular but "lazy" investments that don't historically compensate them for the risks they entail.

- Investors don't understand the effects of expenses and taxes, and therefore allow far too much of their hard-won savings to leak away from them.

- Investors make far-reaching decisions based on whims, emotions, or superficial tips from amateurs, salespeople, and advisers whose financial interests are in conflict with those of their clients.

- In the end, too many investors wind up with too little money and too much emotional stress.

My professional life is dedicated to teaching people how to take care of themselves and their families so they won't wind up with those unfortunate outcomes. Much of this teaching takes place in dozens of retirement workshops that I lead every year. Tens of thousands of investors have found these sessions helpful and stimulating, and I thoroughly enjoy doing every one, whether it lasts for a couple of hours or a whole day. This book contains the most important material from those workshops.

In doing this work over the years, I've met a lot of great people (along with a few who I'd be happy to forget) and I've had a lot of fun. I hope you will find some fun in these pages, too. I hope you'll find the book easy and enjoyable to read, something you'll want to share with somebody else.

Three serious objectives shaped this work: to educate, to stimulate, and to motivate.

Education is essential because there's simply too much data and information available to investors. Much of it is important, but much of it is a combination of noise and sales pitches. I've spent tens of thousands of hours identifying what matters to investors and what doesn't. You'll find the results in these pages.

Stimulation is valuable because it gets people to think. If you go through this book chapter by chapter, I guarantee that you will think in new ways about investing, about psychology, about your money, and about your future.

Motivation is the most important goal, and at the same time the most elusive. If I have only convinced you that there's a better way—yet my words haven't persuaded you to take some action—then I have failed. What you do or don't do, of course, is outside my control, as it should be. I don't know how to directly motivate you except to use words to paint pictures of what is possible and how your life could be. You'll find two direct examples of this in Chapter 2.

If at the end of this book you understand investing in ways that are brand new to you, then I've done my job of education. If you can see the world around you in new ways and think about what you see in new ways, and if some of the stories from this book help you to notice things that you didn't notice before, then I have done my job of stimulation. And if you take action to improve the way you put your financial resources to work for you, then I have done my job of motivation.

If these things happen, then the many hours spent writing this book will have been worthwhile for me. I'm confident that the time you spend with this material will be no less worthwhile for you.

TEN STEPS TO A PERFECT RETIREMENT

The book title promises 10 steps to a perfect retirement, yet the chapters aren't organized quite that way. I'm about to list these 10 steps and point you to where in the book you'll find out about each one.

This list may seem daunting, filled with tasks that would take you months or even years to complete. They might seem more manageable if I share something I've noticed over the past half-dozen or so years of leading workshops for people looking ahead to retirement. Most of the people who come to these workshops can accomplish all 10 of these steps by attending a one-day workshop and then spending 90 minutes with a professional adviser. This book gives you what's in my workshop. If you can manage another 90 minutes with a good adviser (plus the time it takes to do the necessary homework), you'll have all this done.

Step 1: *Determine how much you will need to live on in retirement.* This will tell you how big your portfolio must be when you retire. And that figure will tell you what investment return you need to get there. Chapter 5 tells you how to establish your basic target for the income you'll need from your portfolio. Most investors give this step too little attention. Investors who don't have this information are too often captivated by fear and greed, taking either too much risk or too little risk, depending on what's happening in the markets. This first step is necessarily the foundation for everything that follows.

Step 2: *Determine how much you want to live on in retirement.* In Chapter 5, you'll find out how to establish your living-it-up target. This gives you a second figure for the target size of your portfolio and the return necessary to achieve it. We talk to many clients who, having neglected to take this step, invest as if they must achieve the highest possible return regardless of risk. Often, analysis will show that they can achieve all their goals with much less risk than they thought.

Step 3: *Determine your tolerance for taking risks.* You'll find important insights on this topic throughout the book. Chapter 10 focuses on risk. For every investment you make, you should understand the inherent risks involved and how this investment will affect the overall risk of your portfolio.

Step 4: *Make all your decisions based on what's probable, not what's possible.* From 1995 through 1999, the Standard & Poor's 500 Index compounded at a rate of 28.5 percent a year, leading many people (including plenty who should have known better) to conclude that successful investing was easy. Some investors scoffed at me in 1999 when I refused to give serious consideration to questions like "What's a fund I can count on to make 75 percent a year?" I was dismissed as hopelessly old-fashioned when I suggested investors should aspire to long-term annual growth of 12 percent.

The brief bull market bubble in 1999 showed us that returns of 75 percent were possible. But the bear market of 2000–2003 showed us that 75 percent losses were equally possible. As it turns out, we have more than three quarters of a century of history to show us what's probable. This, not the flash-in-the-pan excitement of a bull market, should be the basis for your planning. That way, you'll have probability working for you, not against you.

Step 5: *Determine the kinds of assets that will give you the returns you need to achieve your goals.* Academics have done years of mind-numbing research—and some have won Nobel Prizes for it—into this very topic. I have distilled that research into five chapters (6 through 10) that tell you what you need to know and what you should do about it. Actually, I think you'll find this is quite interesting material. You'll learn how to add eight equity asset classes to the S&P 500 Index in order to achieve an extra three percentage points of annual return without taking any more risk than that of this popular index.

Step 6: *Combine those assets in the right proportions into a portfolio that's tailored specifically for you.* I show you exactly how to do that in Chapter 12. I name names of the specific funds you should use at Fidelity, Vanguard, T. Rowe Price, and other sources.

Step 7: *Learn to recognize and control the expenses of investing.* Chapter 11 will tell you how to recognize expenses as "leaks" in your portfolio and how to plug them. There are many things about investing that you can't control, but this is one that you can. Savvy investors pay lots of attention to expenses. Sloppy investors would rather not be bothered. Over a lifetime, the difference can add up to tens—or even hundreds—of thousands of dollars.

Step 8: *Make sure you understand enough about the tax laws to avoid giving Uncle Sam a bigger-than-necessary cut of your money.* Lots of investors carelessly squander opportunities and assets because they don't pay attention to tax issues. This is a big topic, but we hit the high spots in Chapter 11. The advice you'll find there will help you turn your investments into an efficient machine that works as hard as possible for you, not the tax man.

Step 9: *Establish the right distribution plan that will give you the income you need in retirement along with the peace of mind of knowing you won't run out of money.* Of all the 10 steps, this one is taught and discussed the least when professionals and authors try to help people handle their money. Investors who bungle this by withdrawing too much too fast can wind up impoverished in their old age—or broke. Investors at the other extreme can, sometimes without realizing it, pass up fantastic opportunities to enjoy life and contribute to others during their lifetimes.

Chapter 13 tells you how to get this step right and gives you much to think about. Among many other things, you'll find a conservative strategy that, based on actual asset returns from recent history, would have multiplied a retiree's annual income by six times over a 30-year retirement; at the end of that 30 years, the portfolio would have been worth more than six times as much as its starting value.

Step 10: *Put everything you do on automatic pilot.* In 40 years of working with people and their money, I've seen again and again the value of making careful, thoughtful decisions and forming those decisions into a plan that can be executed automatically. Investors who do this are likely to achieve the highest returns among their peers at whatever level of risk is appropriate for them.

There are many good ways to do this. Accumulate savings through dollar-cost-averaging. Invest in funds through automatic investment plans that take money out of your bank account regularly or through payroll deduction. Set up your portfolio for automatic rebalancing at the same time every year, using your electronic calendar to remind you if necessary. (This guarantees that you will buy low and sell high.) Fund your IRA in the first week of every year. If you can, do the same with your 401(k) or similar plan at work.

Invest in index funds, which by nature will automatically correct for the unexpected disasters in the market. If a big company goes into the tank unexpectedly (think of Enron), the S&P 500 Index will automatically correct for that with no action required from you. Set up your withdrawals automatically too, so you never have to worry about how much to take out or when. In other words, organize your finances so you don't have to spend a lot of time on them, so they just do what they need to do on your behalf, letting you concentrate on the things that make life worth living.

If you want what my schoolteachers used to call "extra credit," here's an 11th step: *Very carefully, choose and hire a financial adviser.* This is such a valuable move that I've devoted Chapter 14 to it.

If you apply yourself seriously to these 10 steps (and taking the 11th will make the others much easier and more likely to be successful), you will have the best possible chance for that perfect retirement.

A NOTE TO THE READER

Even a casual reader is likely to notice quickly that this book is unusual. This reflects the fact that not everybody learns the same way. It also reflects my personal commitment to make the material in this book as useful as possible and to keep it up to date for you, the reader.

This book is designed to be read at several levels. The simplest level makes it about a 30-page book. Almost every chapter begins with a brief introductory essay that presents the main points in the chapter, without supporting evidence or a full discussion. If you want a general overview of what's in this book, you can get it by reading only those essays. Of course I hope you will want to know more and will take the time to delve into the contents.

The second level is the main text, including graphs, charts, and tables. This is the heart of the book, the stuff that makes it worth your money and your time. The concepts presented here are not complex. If you enjoy reading the business sections of daily newspapers, you should have no trouble following my arguments and the evidence that backs them up.

Along the way you will see some graphs and tables unlike any that you're likely to be familiar with. If you have a little patience, understanding these illustrations won't be hard. They will help you to see information in new ways so that the important points become obvious at a glance.

You'll find the third level throughout the book in the form of highlighted text boxes that act as sidebars to illuminate ideas you might want to come back to for reference. Some of this material does not fit conveniently into the text but is still relevant and helpful. You can skip these boxes without missing the main points of the book. But I hope you'll find them worth your while.

The fourth part of the book is most unusual because it is based on today's technology: a web site (www.wiley.com/go/paul merriman) that was created just for the readers of this book. Here you'll find more detailed versions of some of the charts and tables in the book. You'll also find reference documents that wouldn't fit into these pages as well as links to newsletter articles I published elsewhere.

You'll be able to come back to this web site in the future to see updated material that will always incorporate returns and results from the most recent calendar year. Be sure to visit this site for any updates to our suggested portfolios before you invest. In addition, the web site will give you a chance to submit a question and to read my answers to questions posed by other readers. In the book's appendix you'll learn exactly how to do that.

Finally, the appendix at the end of the book contains my suggestions for further reading and education.

Here's a final important note: I am the founder and president of a company in Seattle that provides investment education, advice, and management. We are in the business of managing money for clients.

My experience as a hands-on money manager gives me an enormous amount of practical experience with real people in real situations. This book is filled with stories and insights based on decades of being "in the trenches" helping investors who in many ways may be like you.

Our business is carefully organized so that we have no conflict of interest with our clients. I have done my best to avoid anything self-serving in this book, and I have asked my editors to hold my feet to the fire in that regard. Still, I definitely have a point of view and some strong beliefs about what serves investors best. I am happy to let you be the final judge. Don't take what I say on blind faith. If you find my views credible, then please use them however you wish.

Part I

■■■■■

Why Some Succeed and Many Fail

■■■■■

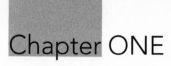

Chapter ONE

Why Investors Fail

If you don't profit from your mistakes, someone else will.

—Yale Hirsch

Investing isn't terribly difficult, but it's a specialized area that requires careful navigation. A huge industry has evolved to use a multitude of clever ways to separate people from part of their retirement savings without necessarily providing much benefit in return. In simple terms, this means that neither your broker nor any of the array of experts on Wall Street is necessarily your friend or even on your side.

Think of investing as a journey. You start at one place and head for another. If you want to drive from California to Michigan quickly and painlessly, there are relatively few choices that make sense. Most will probably draw heavily on the interstate highways. But imagine how hard it would be to plan such a trip if sales forces for several hundred competing highways were giving you tantalizing promises, saying they could get you there better and faster if you would just choose their routes.

Investing is a little bit like that: The best route may be efficient but boring. But along the way there are hundreds of distractions and opportunities to get you off the track. Most investors have a tough time making good investment decisions. They don't have the training or the knowledge. The difficulty of understanding all the options sometimes appears greater than the benefits of doing so. As a result, somewhere along the way almost every investor makes at least one serious mistake. Some never seem to stop making mistakes.

In this chapter we'll look at some of the more serious ways that typical investors work against their own interests. Investors procrastinate or remain passive when the circumstances call for action. They ignore the effects of taxes and expenses. They don't think about their long-term and short-term goals in a clear, organized way. They don't have a written plan for how to get from where they are to where they're going. (Think of it as a road map. If you leave it at home, it's no help.)

Most investors occasionally take way too much risk. Sometimes they don't take nearly as much risk as they should. Investors pay too much of their hard-earned savings to other people who are not necessarily on their side. Too many investors act as if they think smiling salespeople are their friends. They put too much faith in institutions, as if they believe big companies are organized for their customers' benefit. They put too much faith in what they see on financial television, hear on the radio, and read in financial publications. In doing this, they fail to distinguish between facts (which can be very useful) and interpretation, persuasion, and marketing.

Without getting any particular benefit in return, too many investors give up liquidity, making it costly and inconvenient to get their money back when they need it. They have unrealistic expectations and treat investing as a competitive sport. They take investment advice or tips from strangers or amateurs. They invest in ways that fill their emotional needs instead of their financial ones. Thus, they give in to fear and greed, arguably the two most powerful forces on Wall Street. They put their money into investments they don't understand, leading to grief, loss, and disillusionment that sometimes prompts them to give up altogether.

Collectively, that's the bad news. Whew!

The good news is that investing does not have to be that hard. This book will show you precisely how to overcome all those hurdles and how to draw up a road map that's right for you. You'll learn how to implement that plan so that good investment decisions become automatic—instead of random events that happen by luck.

Investing is about taking risks. When you risk your capital, you are entitled to expect a fair return commensurate with the level of risk you take. But if you're not careful, your own mistakes can prevent you from achieving the return that should be yours.

When I meet with a new client, one of the first things we talk about is risk. It's a topic that most of the industry (and most investors) would be happy to avoid altogether. But investors who don't understand risk cannot understand the choices they must make as investors. You'll find numerous references to risks in this book, because it is a critical topic.

Imagine you are in a bank applying for a loan. Suddenly you realize that right at the next desk, Bill Gates is also applying for a loan. Who do you think the bank would rather lend money to? Bill, of course! Don't take it personally, but the bank would always rather lend its money to Bill than to you because there is simply no question about his ability to pay the money back. He's as close to a risk-free, perfect borrower as the bank could wish for. But it's not quite that simple. Bill Gates is not the sort of person who would hesitate to take advantage of his position. If he told the bank he wouldn't pay more than 5 percent interest, and if you were willing to pay 10 percent interest, what do you think the bank would do?

In this case, the bank is in the same position as an investor. It can lend money to Bill and earn 5 percent in a risk-free transaction. Or it can lend money to you and collect twice as much. Obviously the bank would like the extra interest, but how reliable are you? Here's the rub, because the bank can't ever know for sure.

Therefore, the bank must decide if that extra return is worth the extra risk. And that is exactly the challenge that investors face. If you were the banker and you could make only one of those two loans, you'd have to tell your boss either "I turned down Bill Gates for a loan," or "I turned down an opportunity to make twice as much money." Which one would you choose? Would you make that decision on your own without consulting your boss? Probably not!

In real life, bankers have the benefit of institutional and personal experience. They have policies and committees and mentors. They don't have to make decisions like that by the seat of their pants. But much too often, individual investors make variations of this exact same decision without understanding the nature of what they are doing: taking risks that have real consequences.

I usually start my investing workshops by discussing a dozen or so common traps that investors get themselves into. Almost every investor makes at least a few of these mistakes, and I hope you won't feel there's anything wrong with you if some of them sound painfully familiar.

Mistake No. 1: *No written plan*

According to every study I have seen, people with written plans for their investments wind up with much more money during retirement than those who don't have written plans.

This important document should spell out your main assumptions about inflation, future investment returns, how much you'll save before you retire, when you will retire, the amount of money you'll count on from fixed sources such as pensions, Social Security, and perhaps part-time employment, as well as the amount that you'll need to withdraw from your portfolio in retirement. Your written plan should specify how you will make asset allocation choices and where you'll get professional help when you need it.

By the time you finish this book, you'll know the most important things that should be in your written plan. And to give you more specific help, we've put two articles on the web site for this book. One is called "Don't Have an Investment Plan? Start here." Another, written by Rachele Cawaring, is called "Make Your Life Easier with a Written Investment Policy."

Mistake No. 2: *Procrastination*

If you wait for the "right time" to get your investments organized or reorganized, the wait could ruin your results over a lifetime. Procrastination takes many forms. Some people don't start saving for retirement until it's nearly on top of them. Other people know they should review their investments yet always give priority to other things.

Some investors are sure they will catch up later. The irony is that the longer they wait, the less time they have. And time, as anybody who has studied compound interest tables knows, is an investor's best friend. Once you know what you need to do, every day you delay is a day of opportunity that you can never get back.

Mistake No. 3: *Taking too much risk*

In the late 1990s, some relatively inexperienced investors began to act as if they believed investment risk had become only a theoretical concept. But the three-year bear market of 2000 through 2002 was a rude wake-up call to all investors.

Most people understand at least in general that higher risks go along with higher returns. But too many investors act as if they are immune to risk. Or perhaps they believe they will somehow know when it's time to sell a risky investment they bought. Investors typically don't make any up-front effort to understand the nature of the risks they are taking when they make an investment. And they rarely have a plan for what they will do if things don't turn out the way they planned. People who take too much risk often wind up being speculators rather than investors. Savvy investors, on the other hand, pay a lot of attention to limiting and managing risks. If they speculate, they do so with money they know they can afford to lose.

Mistake No. 4: *Taking too little risk*

Some people are paranoid about losing any money at all. They want things nailed down, secure, guaranteed. The majority of money in 401(k) plans, at least until the great bull market of the late 1900s, was invested in guaranteed interest contracts, bonds, money market funds, and similar low-risk securities. Those choices give investors the illusion of short-term security—but in the long run, it's only an illusion.

Especially after the bear market of 2000 to 2002, it may seem important to avoid losses. But that risk is tiny compared with the gains you are likely to give up by avoiding equities. Very-low-risk investments always come packaged with low returns. If your emergency money is in a bank account paying 2 percent interest, you may think there's no risk. But in fact, you are taking the very real risk (in the long term it's a virtual certainty) that inflation and taxes will rob your money of some of its purchasing power.

If you're saving for retirement 25 years down the road, and you opt for a very conservative mix of investments that is expected to return 7 percent annually instead of an all-equity portfolio with an expected annual return of 12 percent, you may be massively short-changing yourself. After 25 years of contributions of $3,000 a year, a 7 percent portfolio will grow to $203,029. But invest the same capital at 12 percent and you will have more than twice as much: $448,002.

Mistake No. 5: *Trusting institutions*

I often ask participants in my workshops if they trust their banks. Most of them answer with a pretty firm "No!" Yet most of us still habitually act as if we believe our banks will tell us if we should move our money in some way that would be more beneficial to us.

You and your bank have a classic conflict of interest. Your best interests are served by an account that pays the highest interest along with penalty-free access to your money whenever you need it. Your bank's best interests are served by accounts that pay you little or no interest. Your bank also wants you to buy products on which it can earn sales commissions, like load mutual funds and various types of insurance.

It's even worse than that. Perhaps the single most profitable thing that banks do is bounce checks on overdrawn accounts. Bankers who work in branches (and thus deal with customers face to face) will be happy to help you manage your money so that you don't bounce checks. But if every checking account customer were bounce-free for a year, billions of dollars in profits would vanish—and some executives in bank headquarters would find themselves looking for jobs.

Because of these conflicts, it's a mistake to rely on a bank to tell you what's in your best interest. The same is true of brokerage houses and insurance companies, too.

Mistake No. 6: *Believing the media*

The headlines on the covers of financial magazines are often predictable: "The Six Best New Funds." "Found: The Next Microsoft." "Everyone's Getting Rich; Here's How to Get Your Share." (Those are actual examples.) The purpose of those headlines is to get you to dive into the contents enough so you'll buy the magazine and see the advertising within. We'll discuss this in more detail in Chapter 4. Here are a couple of high points.

Serious investors need textbooks more than hot ideas. But most people would rather have entertainment, and that's what broadcast outlets and financial publications provide. Writers and editors and publications follow fads. They write about what's in favor and what's in style. When the winds of popularity change, you can bet that they won't be far behind. The purpose of these articles is not to help you. The purpose of the articles is to get you to buy the publications.

The right way to read financial articles that tout specific mutual funds and stocks is to treat those articles as entertainment. The wrong way is to regard them as prescriptions for investment decisions you should make. If you remember that, you might easily save yourself 100 times the cover price of this book.

Mistake No. 7: *Failing to take small steps that can make big differences*

Far too many people fail to make their IRA contributions at the start of the calendar year. Others fail to make IRA contributions at all. They leave money in taxable accounts instead of sheltering it in retirement accounts. They don't maximize their opportunities for corporate matching money in 401(k) and similar plans. They have multiple small IRA accounts, paying annual fees for each one instead of consolidating these assets into a single account that can avoid such fees and make rebalancing easier.

Bank customers, spurred by laziness or inertia or thinking that it doesn't matter, don't move their money from checking accounts into money market deposit accounts. Others don't move their money from money market deposit accounts to nonbank money market funds where they can earn more interest. Each of these steps seems small by itself. Yet over a lifetime they can make a big difference—but only to people who act.

Mistake No. 8: *Buying illiquid financial products*

Liquidity is the ability to get your money back quickly without undue penalties. A stock is very liquid; you can turn it into cash whenever the market is open and you'll have your cash in a few days. Mutual funds are even more liquid, letting you have your cash the following day if you have set up electronic transfers into a bank account. Money market funds and many bond funds give you same-day access to your money by letting you write a check.

But liquidity is severely compromised when you invest in limited partnerships, for which there is often no market. Liquidity is also impaired with variable annuities and shares in load mutual funds that charge penalties for withdrawals made before certain waiting periods have expired.

Some people sink their rainy day savings into their homes by making extra principal payments on their mortgages. But when that rainy day comes along, the only way to "withdraw" that extra principal may be to refinance (a time-consuming, expensive process) or sell the home. (And if you're facing financial troubles, your refinancing prospects could be at a low point.)

Mistake No. 9: *Requiring perfection in order to be satisfied*

People who can't stand to have anything but "the best" solution seldom make successful investors. No matter where you put your money, there will always be something that's performing better than what you have. And if you're lucky enough to own the one fund that's doing better than everything else, you can be certain it won't remain that way for long. That's just the nature of this business.

Perfectionists often flit from one thing to the next, chasing elusive performance. In real life, you get a premium for risk only if you stay the course. If you demand perfect investments, you never will.

Mistake No. 10: *Accepting investment advice and referrals from amateurs*

If you had a serious illness, I hope you would consult a nurse or a doctor, not somebody on the street who happened to have an opinion or what you should do—or worse, somebody who had a product to sell you. I hope you would treat your life savings and your financial future with the same care as you'd treat your health. Sad to say, too many people make financial decisions based on things they hear casually. The lure of the "hot tip" is all but irresistible to some investors. But as painful as it is, there are no safe shortcuts to wealth.

A client once told me he had heard about a woman who "made a lot of money" for some of his friends. My client, normally a very conservative man, cashed in $250,000 of his portfolio and turned it over to this woman, who told him she would invest it in "a conservative strategy." Within two months, she had lost half his money. Only then did this client investigate enough to learn that she was not even licensed to do what she was doing. Her compensation was to be 20 percent of whatever profits he made. That gave her an incentive to generate big profits quickly. Unfortunately for my client, she had no disincentive to take big risks—because all the risks were his.

Mistake No. 11: *Letting emotions drive investment decisions*

The two most powerful forces that drive decisions on Wall Street are emotional: fear and greed. Think about this the next time you listen to a radio or television commentator explaining what's happening in the stock market. You'll hear echoes of fear and greed over and over.

Some investors fear rising interest rates; others fear falling interest rates. Some fear inflation while others welcome it. You name it, somebody's afraid of it. Fear is why so many investors bail out of carefully planned investment strategies when things look bleak. Investors sell en masse when prices are down; that reduces their profits or increases their losses.

Greed, likewise, blinds investors and makes them forget what they should know. In the last half of 1999 and the first half of 2000, greed prompted many investors to stuff their portfolios with high-flying technology stocks. But in the spring of 2000, most of those stocks plunged without warning. This quickly transformed many greedy investors into fearful investors.

The desire to make money is legitimate. But unless it is tempered with a healthy respect for risk, it turns into greed. Likewise, the desire to avoid or limit losses is legitimate. But when it is allowed to run amok, it turns into fear.

Mistake No 12: *Putting too much faith in short-term performance*

Many investors, especially inexperienced ones, spend far too much time and energy trying to forecast what essentially cannot be forecast: short-term performance. Worse, they give far too much credence to recent short-term performance. We tend to think that whatever just happened will continue to happen. Sometimes that's true, but a lot of the movement in the stock market is essentially random. That's one reason recent performance is a lousy predictor of future performance.

Mistake No. 13: *Overconfidence*

Many investors get into trouble when they start believing that they really know what they are doing. They become overconfident. There's an old saying on Wall Street to the effect that every 1 percent increase in a bull market makes investors think their IQs have gone up a point.

Many overconfident investors put too much of their money into a single stock or a single fund. Then they get emotionally attached, and their attachment takes on a life of its own. Investors' overconfidence tends to persist even when a favored investment starts heading downward. By the time such an investor is finally willing to admit that things have changed, he or she will probably have stayed much too long.

Mistake No. 14: *Focusing on the wrong things*

We'll talk a lot in this book about asset allocation, which is the choice of what kind of assets go into your portfolio. It's generally accepted that asset allocation accounts for more than 90 percent of investors' returns. That leaves less than 10 percent for choosing specific stocks and mutual funds—the very thing on which most investors spend almost all their time and energy.

Even when investors have properly allocated their portfolios, they can look at the wrong things. This happens when they focus on small parts of their portfolios instead of the whole package. They can become obsessed with a small investment that seems to stubbornly refuse to do its part during a bull market. In fact, it's normal and expected for investments to go down as well as up, even during a bull market. That's what makes it possible to "buy low," an essential part of buying low and selling high. But sometimes an enraged investor will overthrow an entire portfolio because of what happens to some small part of it.

This wouldn't be such a problem if investors had a better understanding of diversification. The whole point of diversification is to always have some things in a portfolio that "aren't working." That's because whatever is performing well at a given time won't necessarily continue to do so. And when that happens, you want some other asset class waiting in the wings to have its day in the sun, so to speak.

Mistake No. 15: *Needing proof before making a decision*

This is a variation of Mistakes No. 2, procrastination, and No. 9, requiring perfection. The ultimate stalling tactic for investors who aren't ready to make a move is to require one more piece of information or evidence. You can get evidence for just about any view of the market you want, but you cannot get proof. You can prove what happened in the past, but there's no way to prove anything about the future. It has always struck me as ironic that the main focus of mutual fund advertising is past performance, yet that's the one thing that the funds can't sell and investors can't buy.

If you must have certainty, stick to Treasury bills and certificates of deposit. If you're seeking returns higher than those, you will have to accept some uncertainty. The only certain thing about the future is that it won't look just like the past. Savvy investors who understand that will hedge their bets by diversifying. Remember, investors get paid to take calculated risks. They can't do that if they must know in advance how things are going to turn out.

Mistake No. 16: *Not knowing how to deal with the first 15 mistakes*

The cures for all these mistakes may seem obvious, but they are not necessarily easy. They boil down to education, discipline, and managing your emotions. Throughout this book you will find hundreds of ways that should help you do just that.

Here are a few thoughts right now, while all this investment carnage is fresh in your mind.

- Make sure you have a written investment plan—even if it's only on a single piece of paper—that outlines what you must do to achieve your long-term and short-term goals. Use specific measurable interim goals so you can keep track of your progress.

- Educate yourself. Finish this book and continue learning from the suggested reading list in the Appendix and from the article library on the web site for this book.

- If you don't understand an investment, don't put your money into it. I believe this single step will prevent more grief than almost anything else you can do.

▓ Sometimes the best course may be to simply slow down. Take a deep breath and apply a liberal dose of patience. It's probably the most underrated virtue I know in this fast-paced world.

▓ Finally, if you notice that emotions are driving your decisions, substitute a discipline. If you have trouble finding or implementing a proper discipline, consider professional investment advice or money management.

In the end, the best one-word prescription for avoiding most mistakes is diversification.

Chapter TWO

Stress versus Success:
A Tale of Two Investors

Content makes poor men rich. Discontent makes rich
men poor.

—Benjamin Franklin

There's a big difference between people who get retirement
right and those who get it wrong. This difference is a combination (in rough order of importance) of attitude, habits,
mental clarity, discipline, diligence, determination, and a
lifetime of cumulative choices. Oh, and good luck doesn't
hurt; but don't rely on it.

Most of us make choices all the time that will help determine whether our retirement years are golden or gloomy.
Whether you're planning your retirement in the future, on
the verge of retiring, or already retired, you'll stack the odds
in your favor if you learn what separates successful retirees
from those who are doomed to struggle.

You might learn these things from reading lists of smart moves and dumb moves. But you're more likely to remember a picture of success contrasted with a picture of struggle. In this chapter I'll introduce you to two of my long-time clients, whom I'll call George and Roger. In the following chapter, we'll take a list-based look at this topic.

George seems to have done everything right. Roger has done so many things wrong that I hate to think what his life must be like. I've changed the names and a few biographical details to protect these people's identities. Otherwise, the following is true and accurate.

George

If you could meet George Caldwell, a former Army officer and surgeon, I'm almost certain you would like him. The same goes for his wife, Ruth, an accomplished musician with a charming personality. After he left the service as a lieutenant colonel, George went into private practice for 14 years as a surgeon.

By agreement between George and Ruth, the first claim on their income every year was to make the maximum allowed contribution to a tax-deferred retirement plan. "We saved first, and what we had left over was what we could live on," he said.

Even though they had more than enough for a comfortable life, George and Ruth made a point of living below their means. "My friends were driving Jaguars and Mercedes, but we didn't. We drove Hondas, and I still drive a used Honda. We didn't play big shots, because that wasn't important to us. We lived in a house that was very modest compared to everybody we knew." George and Ruth always shopped for the best deal on everything they bought, and they never felt deprived. Ruth can afford to drive any car she wants. Last time I checked in with her, she was driving an 11-year-old economy sedan.

While he was working, George dabbled at investments and once had a fairly complicated strategy that required him to watch the market every business day. Once when he was out of the country he left his paperwork at home and could not keep up with his systems. He lost more than $6,000. He remembers the lesson much more than the money he lost. He later consolidated all his accounts into a simpler strategy that has Ruth's blessing. Though she leaves investment decisions to him, "I run big decisions past her in advance because she has a lot of good sense," George said. "When we disagree on something, we work it out until we are both satisfied."

A frugal lifestyle and conservative investments mean they can live the life they want. She pursues music, he pursues travel and other interests. To fund a major three-month trip to Antarctica, George didn't raid the couple's retirement portfolio. Instead they simply cut back on other expenses for awhile.

George's formula sounds easy: Make a bundle of money, save a lot of it, and keep your spending down. But doing this has required careful, deliberate choices between what is important to them and what is not. They have set realistic investment goals. And they've managed to avoid the disagreements and power struggles that derail many people's financial plans.

I asked George what he would recommend to somebody who was about to retire. "I'd say you have to do some figuring. Look at what you have and what you'll need. Examine your lifestyle and what it will cost you. Be sure to account for inflation." He'd recommend a book he gave to his children, "The Armchair Millionaire" by Lewis Schiff, Douglas Gerlach, and Kate Hanley.

Roger

Roger Bell, on the other hand, constantly struggles with his money, his investments, and his emotions. He's been an on-again, off-again client of our firm. Frankly we have taken him back several times against our better judgment, hoping he will get his life straightened out. But his pattern continues. He opens an account, gets frustrated, loses his patience, and then fires us. Sometime later, almost like clockwork, he calls us back saying he needs our help because he can't stand what happens when he manages his own money. He tells us this time he has learned his lesson and things will be different.

Like George, Roger retired with what would seem to be plenty of money to live a good life. But he suffered a series of significant investment losses as he followed his own investment whims. The losses resulted not from choosing bad strategies, but from repeatedly shifting from one investment "plan" to another, never giving any strategy enough time to work properly. Against our advice, Roger is essentially addicted to chasing recent hot per-formance, trying to find a spectacularly successful investment that will let him recover his past losses. And as the losses accu-mulate, recovery becomes harder and harder to achieve.

When he has been our client, Roger has invested in sensible strategies that are likely to meet his needs over the long run. But he can't seem to accept short-term setbacks and has never been patient enough to let long-term strategies work. Ironically, Roger's fear of not making enough money has led him to make investments in which he has lost a lot of money. Intellectually, Roger understands all this. But he can't get the emotional part of it right.

When we manage Roger's money, he is constantly watching for anything that he perceives as a mistake. When he manages his own money, he is either wildly overconfident (when his lat-est investment has gone up in value) or quite depressed (when his latest investment has gone down). Roger does not have any long-term plan I'm aware of. He hasn't figured out his risk tolerance. And as far as I know, over the past 12 years he has lost more money than he has gained. On the outside, his life looks prosperous. He drives a nice car, lives in a nice home, and has a fabulous boat. But on the inside, his anxiety over his finances poisons his ability to be satisfied.

Roger's wife, Joyce, has a separate account that we manage for her without any input from her husband. She has much more patience and a long-term attitude. It's no surprise that she's more successful. But when we talk to Roger, we don't hear many happy stories about his life. Roger's approach to his money has led to some serious fights with Joyce, who has found it nearly impossible to be a supportive partner to him.

Even after the losses he has taken, Roger still could live quite comfortably, even if he put all his money into certificates of deposit, which I have suggested to him. But he doesn't. In the end, Roger's money has become a problem for him instead of a tool to give him a life that he wants to live.

I hope this book will help you be more like George and less like Roger!

Chapter THREE

Lessons from Smart People

▪▪▪▪▪▪

What the wise do in the beginning, fools do in the end.

—Warren Buffett

Successful retirement requires something more than just raw financial numbers. That's obvious from the stories of George and Roger, the two retirees we met in Chapter 2 and who each ended their working lives with more than enough money yet wound up in very different places. Left to their own devices, most people will wind up somewhere between the two opposites of George, who seems to have done just about everything right, and Roger, who has not managed to have a successful retirement in spite of starting out with plenty of money.

In four decades of helping and watching people manage their money, before and during retirement, I've had a chance to observe how the smartest people I know deal with retirement. It boils down to this: Smart people take a thoughtful, long-term approach to their lives. They avoid extremes, more often than not choosing middle-of-the-road investment strategies. They regard their money as a tool, not as the center of their lives. They have plenty of things to live for and they look for ways to connect positively with other people.

Smart Step 1

Smart people make plans for their retirement, financial and otherwise, and they put those plans in writing. It has always puzzled me why people will spend days planning a two-week vacation (and in some cases months planning a half-day wedding and reception) yet those same people will make five-figure and even six-figure investment decisions on a whim. An article published in *Fortune Magazine* in 1999 described a study that found investors who made written plans by the time they were 40 wound up on average with five times as much money by age 65 as those who didn't have written plans.

Of course the act of writing a plan doesn't put money in anybody's pocket. And even the most brilliant plan is worthless if it collects dust on a shelf. But people who are methodical enough to put their plans into writing are also likely to do many of the other things that lead to successful investing. That's one of the key points of this book: A successful retirement doesn't result from one or two acts of genius; it results from many actions and habits cultivated over the years. With a written plan, you can get back on course when you go astray. Without a plan, you don't even have a reliable way to determine whether you are off course.

Smart Step 2

Smart people, before and during retirement, don't spend much of their time on the proverbial porch rocking in the proverbial chair. Instead they keep themselves active and challenged, both mentally and physically. It's no secret that people who use their brains live longer than those who are intellectually lazy. There are lots of enjoyable ways to do this, including reading, crossword puzzles, and taking (or teaching) a class. Travel is another excellent way to keep the mind and body in good shape. The smartest and happiest people I know are invariably interested and curious about many things. They never stop wanting to learn new ways to understand the world and interact with it.

Physical activity is also a great way to enhance your retirement. Whether it's climbing mountains or just walking around the block, smart people remain physically active to whatever extent they can.

Smart Step 3

Smart people cultivate new relationships and nurture their established ones with friends, family, and colleagues. I've worked with many retired people and I've noticed that the happiest ones seem to have many favorite people in their lives, including people younger than they are. These happy retirees are invariably interested in other people and seem to take a delight in finding ways to do favors, not for credit or appreciation but for the satisfaction of being able to help make life better for somebody else.

At the end, life can sweep away our dignity and our money.

But if we have friends with whom we can share joy, pain, and re-spect, we are blessed. This is something that money cannot buy.

Smart Step 4

Smart people have lots to live for. They wouldn't have any trou-ble making a list of two dozen things they would like to do if they had time. Places to go. People to see. Books to read. New things to learn.

Smart Step 5

Smart investors and retirees pay attention to their money and treat it as if it were precious. This seems so obvious that you may wonder why I'd bother to mention it in a book like this. Here's why: I've seen too many people, including ones with high incomes, treat money as a if it were an unlimited resource, almost like water flowing into their lives at the twist of a tap. These people seem to barely notice when money leaves their pockets.

Thomas Stanley, chairman of the Affluent Market Institute in Atlanta, has spent 30 years studying wealthy people and how they got that way. He observed that the typical wealthy person is likely to have lived in the same city for many years and to live in a middle-class neighborhood next door to people much less wealthy. Stanley says great wealth builders spend plenty of time planning their investments. They would rather spend money on good financial advice than on a new boat. The least effective wealth builders are those who turn their important financial de-cisions over to other people.

The key word in that last sentence is "decisions." I believe most investors can benefit from professional advice and man-agement. But nobody can give you the best advice or manage-ment unless you have made some critical decisions about the risks you are willing to take and how you will manage those risks. If you delegate such important choices to somebody else, you are inviting mistakes that can lead to major disappointments and bitterness—and the possible derailment of your long-term objectives.

I'd like you to spend as much time as it takes to understand your investment needs and establish a plan that will make your money work hard for you. And then I'd like you to set that plan on "automatic pilot" so you can concentrate on enjoying life.

Smart Step 6

Smart people don't wait for luck to make them wealthy (see box). Instead, they cultivate habits and attitudes that improve the odds of their success. They spend less than they can afford to on vacations, houses, cars, and entertainment. They put their money to work building wealth, not building lifestyles that saddle them with expenses and debt.

One of the best quotes on luck I ever heard was from talk show host Dave Ramsey: "Good things happen to people who are doing all the right things. That is how luck gets created."

My own take on luck is this: Things happen that people regard simply as good luck. But something transforms a random event into an opportunity. If you're able to recognize a circumstance as an opportunity, and if you're prepared to take advantage of it, then it's a lucky break. But if the same thing happened to somebody else who didn't recognize it as an opportunity, or who didn't have the resources or the ability to capitalize on it, then it's just a random event without meaning.

> If you "do all the right things," you'll improve your chances of getting a lucky break. And ironically, if you're doing all the right things, you won't have so much need for that lucky break.

Smart Step 7

Smart people who are planning retirement don't short-change themselves and their futures. They don't buy the notion they will be able to get by on only 70 percent of their preretirement income. They have lots of things they want to do, and they want the means to fully participate in everything they can. Many of my clients spend more during retirement than they did while they were working—and when it doesn't jeopardize their future plans, I encourage them to do it.

Smart Step 8

Smart people don't burden themselves with a heap of consumer debt. Sure, most folks need credit to buy a house, which can turn out to be a fine investment. And most working people need loans to buy vehicles. But revolving credit is like a nasty drug habit that keeps people enslaved and prevents them from being independent.

Credit cards aren't inherently bad. If you can pay off your balance every month, you can get some nice freebies, whether it's frequent flyer miles, a cash rebate, or a donation to a favorite charity. But if you just make the payments, you'll probably be sorry. And you'll almost certainly forget what you spent the money on before it's paid for. With a credit card and a free-spending attitude, it's easy to rack up a balance of $3,000 in an afternoon. Even if you never charge another dime, at a typical monthly payment rate of 2 percent of the balance coupled with an annual interest rate of 16.5 percent, it could take you 30 years—and payments of nearly $8,500—to finally pay for that $3,000 spending spree.

Smart Step 9

Smart people know the value of time, and they don't wait until the last minute to start planning for retirement. If you're in your twenties, retirement seems pretty remote. Yet that's exactly the point: All that time is what gives you the opportunity to do a lot with a little.

If you can manage to contribute $3,000 every year into a Roth IRA starting when you're 25, and if you get a 12 percent return (roughly the long-term average rate of the stock market), by age 60 you'll have roughly $1,450,000. But if you wait until you're 40 to start making those contributions, you'll have only about $245,000 when you're 60. If you look at it another way, a one-time investment of $5,000 when you're 25 will grow (at 12 percent) to $263,998 by the time you're 60. Wait until you're 40 and you'll have to start with $27,368 to get the same result. Wait until you're 50, and you'll have to start with $85,000.

Smart Step 10

Smart people who have waited too long don't try to play catch-up by investing in high-risk ventures that rely on luck to make up for lost time. Instead, they find ways to save more and scale back their retirement needs. If necessary, they plan to work longer while they build their assets in a sensible way. If they take extra investment risk, they do so thoughtfully and carefully.

Risk is a central topic that deserves investors' attention, and it's worthy of another thoughtful discussion here. The markets reward investors who assume prudent risks, and the way you handle this will have a big impact on how successful you are as a long-term investor.

Most of us have no direct control over the external events that affect our investments. But we can control how we respond to them. To a greater or lesser extent, all of us struggle internally in a battle between intellect and emotion —between our fear and greed on the one hand and our discipline and reason on the other. Very few among us are so disciplined that our reason always rules our actions. This plays out in the stock market every day. Because we must invest for a future that we cannot know, there is simply no way we can escape taking risks.

Here's something I wrote to my company's clients in 1998 and again in 2000, in both cases when the market had unexpectedly turned downward: "In the good times, it seems as if investing is about *accepting wealth.* You put down your money, almost like planting it in a garden, and watch it grow. But in fact, in good times and bad, investing is really about *managing risk and managing your emotions.* To be a successful investor, you have to do at least a decent job at both those tasks."

Managing risk is the hardest part of investing. The best way to start is to understand what risk really is. Mathematical definitions of risk are good for measuring and comparing risks. But they don't get at the heart of how real people actually experience risk. The *American Heritage Dictionary* defines risk as "the possibility of suffering harm or loss." Other definitions use the words *danger, uncertainty,* and *hazard.*

Here's my own definition: *Risk is a possibility that you invite into your life in which you could lose something important.*

That something could be your physical safety, a relationship, or money.

Let me use an analogy. When you invite a guest into your home, you are taking some level of risk. There's always the possibility that your guest could take something or damage something or be rude to you or your family or other guests if you have them. Experience may make you pretty sure this won't happen, but it is a possibility, and you are the one who invited that guest.

My definition of risk, while unconventional, is carefully crafted to make a couple of important points. The word *invite* makes it quite clear that risk is not imposed on you from the outside. On the contrary, it results from a choice you make. You choose to invite someone into your home. Likewise, prudent investment risk is something you accept and knowingly choose.

Second, this definition makes it clear that risk is not theoretical. We'll measure it in this book in terms of statistics. But risk is about actually losing something important. (I wish more teenage drivers understood this concept!)

Why would anybody willingly take the risk of losing something important? Because that's what investors get paid to do. In general, the more risk you are willing to take, the more return you may possibly receive. However, this is true only when you take intelligent risks based on understanding. It doesn't apply to random risks based on bravado or recent hot performance.

There are two categories of risk: objective risk, which can be measured, and emotional risk, which depends on each person's perceptions.

Imagine you are shopping for a certificate of deposit (CD). The easiest place to get a CD is your own bank. But it's highly unlikely that your bank just happens to have the very best deal in the country. If you want to do business with the folks down the block who know you, you'll have to accept whatever interest rate your bank pays. On the other hand, you can shop around and perhaps find a higher interest rate at a bank 1,000 miles away.

Objectively, the risk is identical. Each CD is guaranteed by the U.S. government. But the distant bank may hold more emotional risk. You can't walk into a branch and talk to the manager. You may never know anybody there except by phone. But because the distant bank pays higher interest, you are in effect earning a premium return for the small amount of emotional risk you take by banking there.

It's easy to measure the risk of past investments, as we discuss in some detail in Chapter 11. After the fact, it's pretty easy to say, "I could handle that," because you know how it turned out. But when you contemplate the next 30 years, you're looking risk straight in the eyes, because you have no idea what's ahead. That's why I often say, "There's no risk in the past. The only risk is in the future."

Getting risk right is a balancing act. Take too much, and you can compromise your future by incurring big losses that you can't afford. Take too little, and you can compromise your future by depriving yourself of the return you need.

To determine if you are taking enough risk, ask yourself this: Are my investments providing the return that I need to meet my goals, with a margin left over for error? If the answer is yes, you are probably taking enough risk and don't need to take more.

To determine whether you have assumed too much risk, ask yourself three questions:

1. Have I lost any sleep over my investments?

2. Do I feel compelled to watch the financial news and check fund prices daily or weekly? (We are talking about feeling compelled, not just curious.)

3. Does the financial news make me worry about my future?

If your answer to any of those questions is yes, you may have taken on too much risk. If you answer yes to all three, your investments are definitely too risky for you.

Smart Step 11

Smart people learn from the mistakes of other people so they don't have to repeat them. Virtually everything I've put into this book is based on mistakes I've seen people make. If you learn the lessons here, their pain can become your gain.

Smart Step 12

I think I've saved the best lesson for last. This may seem to contradict everything you've read so far, but it fits. Smart people don't wait for retirement to start making their dreams come true. Smart people accept the fact that life is uncertain and all the tomorrows we assume will be there can be snatched away in an instant. With wealth set aside for their futures and with their goals and dreams clearly identified, the really smart folks I know are always looking for ways to turn those dreams into reality, starting now.

Here's an exercise: Imagine you have somehow acquired a huge amount of money, and you'll never have to work again. The interesting question in this exercise is not how you'd spend your money but how you'd spend your time—because that in essence is your life.

Now write down four or five major things you would like to devote time and energy to for the rest of your life. Maybe it's going back to school, learning how to fly a plane, or honing your skills at a hobby or avocation. Maybe you'd love to be a philanthropist or live in a foreign culture and learn a new language. The object is to identify what you'd do if you could do anything. Then find ways to pursue those interests now. Do it for immediate satisfaction and as preparation for when you'll have more time. For almost anything on your list, you can find ways to indulge your passion without waiting for retirement. If you do that, you'll improve your quality of life now—and after you have retired.

Chapter FOUR

The Psychology of Successful Investing

■■■■■

We are what we repeatedly do. Excellence, then, comes not from our actions but from our habits.

—Aristotle

It's relatively easy to prescribe an investment plan that is likely to work well if it's followed diligently. Much of this book is devoted to doing just that. The hard part is keeping yourself from derailing your own plans. One of the biggest mistakes investors make is underestimating the power of their emotions. If you take the time to understand the psychology of successful investing, you'll make your life more pleasant and you'll probably have more money to spend in retirement and leave to your heirs. But if you ignore this topic, I promise you will pay for doing so.

Many investors get in and out of the stock market from time to time depending on whether they think prices are relatively high or relatively low. Some have mechanical timing systems to guide them, but many people believe they can successfully make their own decisions about when to get in and when to get out. In hindsight, the majority of such moves are counterproductive.

When stock prices are relatively high, financial risk is also high and the opportunity for gains relatively low. Yet high prices, ironically, mean low emotional risk for investors. People find it easy to buy investments that have been going up. On the other hand, when prices are relatively low, financial risk is also low; the opportunity for gains is high. But low prices mean high emotional risk. Again ironically, investors find it hard to buy low-priced investments that have been beaten up in the market and whose near-term prospects seem bleak.

There's no getting around one very basic truth about investing: The way to make money is to buy low and sell high. But our emotions, by trying to bring us comfort, work against us and try to persuade us to do the opposite. In the short run, comfort is very gratifying. But in the long run, comfort always has a cost.

Investors who crave quick, easy answers and peace of mind should expect lower long-term returns. Think about diet and exercise. It's no great mystery how to eat sensibly and exercise regularly. There's little dispute that doing so makes people healthier, happier, and likely to live longer. But knowing the right things to do is not enough. To get results you must somehow get yourself to do the right things, while you avoid doing counterproductive things.

Psychology is the key. If you just do what you feel like,

you'll most likely eat too much, you'll eat the wrong things, and you won't exercise as you should. What "feels good" at the moment is usually a lousy guide to what's really in your best interest. This is just as true of investing as eating.

Throughout your life as an investor, you will be goaded by the media, which will do its best to keep stimulating you with entertainment that's carefully disguised to look like insight and advice. The aim of the media is not to help you. It's to keep you coming back for more—to deliver your attention to advertisers. Unless you realize this, you will be constantly misled.

You can be sure that the investment profession understands psychology very well. If you let them, investment professionals will be only too happy to take advantage of you. Wall Street doesn't really care how you invest your money. The industry's primary goal is to get you to change whatever you're doing. That's how Wall Street makes money. To that end, investors are barraged night and day with sales pitches, some obvious and some masquerading as objective investment advice or insight. All of it is designed to get people to buy and sell. To be a successful investor, you'll have to figure out how to deal with all that.

Investing is in some ways like driving a car. The route you need to take may be pretty straightforward, but your attitude, skills, and psychological makeup will play a major role in shaping your actual experience of the journey. When it's your money at stake, you should be the one in the driver's seat, even if you are taking directions from someone else. The best way to keep your hands on the wheel is to have a plan that will work for you and then stick to it. The best way to do that is to know the difference between your financial needs and your emotional needs.

If you are an investor, I promise that from time to time you will experience setbacks, confusion, frustration, uncertainty, anxiety, and disappointment. How you respond to events and to your emotions will have a big impact on your success, or lack of it. Your investment plan will be more likely to succeed if it is designed to use your psychological strengths and overcome your weak spots. This chapter will show you some useful tools to keep your emotions from leading you down the wrong path. However, only you can apply those tools and keep yourself on the right path.

Ultimately, the solution to many investors' psychological challenges is pretty simple. Because your emotions will never be a reliable guide, your best bet is to put it all on automatic. That means automatic savings, automatic investing, automatic asset allocation, automatic rebalancing, and automatic distributions in retirement.

There's an interesting parallel between the way people drive and the way they invest their money. Good drivers practice defensive driving techniques. If you know what to look out for on the highway, you can greatly improve your chances of getting to your destination safely.

I want you to be a good defensive investor. To do that, there are three things you need to watch out for: your own emotions, the manipulations of Wall Street, and the misleading media. On one level, investing is about knowing the right things to do, then doing them. We will see in this book exactly how to do that.

But in the real world, investors are driven more by emotions than logic. Mark Hulbert, a *New York Times* and *CBSMarketwatch* columnist whose business has been to study investment newsletters since 1980, said it well during an interview on my Internet radio show: "Our intellect is basically no match for our emotions. As we see over and over, emotions will trump the intellect almost every single time."

As an investor, your emotional adversaries are likely to be fear, greed, impatience, and frustration. How you deal with them will have a huge effect on how much money you are at risk of losing. Impatience can be deadly.

In traffic jams, impatient drivers often pay lots of attention to what lane they are in and how other lanes are doing in relation to theirs. If the other lane seems to be moving faster, they will often swerve over to cut in front of somebody else. Some drivers do this repeatedly, taking every opportunity to gain some small advantage for themselves. Those drivers may gain a few seconds. But in the process, they raise the level of danger and annoyance to themselves and everybody around them. In investment terms, drivers like that take on much more risk in return for uncertain (and often elusive) gains.

Impatient investors often watch the market like hawks. They want results, and they want them now. Impatient investors are easy prey for the investment industry. They can be lured to change lanes, then change lanes again, always seeking a competitive advantage. Unfortunately they often wind up as "road kill," retiring to the shoulder of the road with their capital in money market funds while their more patient counterparts build wealth in the slower lane.

Patient investors may wait for decades before they reap their rewards. But they are more likely to be able to retire comfortably—and more likely to sleep better along the way. So here's a piece of advice that may be worth remembering: Every time you invest some money, remind yourself to invest some patience along with it. You will be rewarded.

YOUR STYLE IN THE DRIVER'S SEAT

When you drive, you have a certain style. You may not notice your style, but I promise you that the people who ride with you do. There's a certain amount of frustration you are willing to tolerate from other drivers who don't behave as you think they should. And there's a way you react when that frustration exceeds your limit.

On a clogged freeway, do you weave from lane to lane or rush to the next exit hoping to find a better route that other drivers haven't discovered? Many people change their investments mainly to relieve frustration. The odds of success are not in their favor.

WATCH OUT FOR YOUR EXPECTATIONS

An important part of dealing with your emotions is managing your expectations. Of course you want to make money from your investments. And if you follow a sound investment plan, you will. But I can guarantee this: You won't make money all the time. Unless your investments are limited to Treasury bills or other cash equivalents, your investments at some point will go down in value. What matters is not whether that happens but how you deal with it.

In fact, you should hope you don't make big gains on your investments right away. The reason is psychological, not financial. If you make a lot of money quickly after you invest in something, it will almost always be a random event. But to your mind, that random event will seem very important if it happens in the first hours, days, or weeks of your investment. I've observed over the years that investors are much more likely to stick with investments that "reward" them very early in the game. If a fund shoots up 10 or 20 percent in the first six months you own it, at some level you will develop an emotional bond with it. This bond will cloud your judgment. No longer will this fund be merely a tool that you use to accomplish something. Instead, it will have become an ally or a friend, something you feel you can "trust" to take care of you.

On the other hand, even the best investment plan in the world can have very little emotional appeal if it loses money in the first six months that you own it. You will develop an emotional aversion. You'll start to regard this investment not as a tool but as a bad idea, a sort of adversary that gives you bad vibes.

Here's another trick your mind may play on you: Wall Street spends hundreds of millions of dollars every year to try to make you put your trust in "safe" names that seem familiar and dependable. If the Janus Fund is mentioned in the media in a favorable light enough times, millions of people will have a positive impression of it, even though most of them could not explain why. And this impression has staying power.

From 1970 through 1992, Janus Fund achieved a 16 percent compound rate of return. That and the resulting publicity helped it become one of the nation's largest growth funds in the mid-1990s. Long after this fund's performance fell, its favorable impression persisted and money kept pouring in. Not until the bear market of 2000–2002 did the popular perception of the Janus Fund finally fall into line with the reality that this flagship offering was, at best, an average long-term performer.

YOUR GOALS SHOULD BE GOOD

One of your most important psychological allies will be a set of smart, sensible goals. Many people say their objective is to beat the market. But I don't really believe that, and I'll tell you why. If all you want is to beat the market, then in a year when the market (however you define it) is down 40 percent, you should be supremely happy to lose "only" 35 percent of your money. Do you know anybody who would brag to his or her family about losing 35 percent? I don't. In a good year, if the market is up 30 percent, you'd be compelled to complain to your family if your portfolio went up only 25 percent as if you were a failure.

If you aren't clear about your objectives, you can experience anxiety no matter what results you get. To investors, anxiety is a powerful force that can tempt you to switch investments when you shouldn't.

Veteran investors know that the market does not reward all investors at the same time. Older investors should want higher stock prices so they can convert their investments into cash for living expenses. Younger investors should want lower prices so they can buy a piece of the future at a reduced price.

What should your objective be? There's no right answer for everyone. The only wrong answer is to have no answer, or to believe that you can and should achieve every possible financial goal at the same time.

WATCH OUT FOR WALL STREET

Even when you have your own emotions under control, you've still got to deal with Wall Street. Managing risks is at the heart of successful investing, and you should always focus your attention on this when you're considering a new investment. But you'll rarely find an investment adviser who wants you to do that. The investment industry has learned that when people confront the emotions associated with losing money, most folks will flee before a salesperson can make a dime in commissions.

The industry doesn't want to talk about preparing you for the inevitable bad times, even though that is what you need. The industry just wants to make money while there's money to be made. That happens when commissions are generated, and that happens when you do something. Optimism sells, and it's no accident that Wall Street is organized to make you think higher returns are just a transaction away. If you just sit tight, nobody makes much money. Everybody in the business has a better idea for what you should do with your money, and they're all eager to do it for you.

As investors, we can choose every day from thousands of mutual funds, thousands of managers, thousands of individual stocks as well as many other financial products and plans. It's easy to be a frequent trader. If you wake up in the middle of the night with an investment idea or fear, you can find a broker who will execute a trade for you immediately on the Tokyo or London exchanges.

The industry is highly motivated and highly trained (to say nothing of highly compensated) to do whatever it takes to get your money under management. Competition is fierce, and the sales and marketing forces will use every trick they can to lure you to sign on the dotted line.

There is an exception—and it is not necessarily to your advantage. Very few brokers and investment managers are completely immune to the pain of investing. Not many of them like to have to deal with clients who have sustained major losses. But even this compassion, if you want to call it that, works against investors. Brokers and portfolio managers sometimes shy away from delivering the bad news to clients. And that in turn can mean clients don't act to cut their losses when they should. We saw the effects of this type of denial and inaction during the bear market of 2000 through 2002. Hundreds of thousands of investors failed to protect themselves while their technology-heavy stock portfolios eroded. In many cases, people's retirement dreams were shattered.

> When people are in severe pain, whether it's physical, emotional, or financial, they often lose the ability to make good decisions. Stopping the hurt can become the top priority, sometimes regardless of consequences that will show up later.
>
> Investing money should be about ultimate consequences, not about feeling good today. Many investors act as if the opposite were true. Decisions based on pain and emotions are almost always counterproductive. That's one reason it's

extremely valuable to have a plan you can turn to when things start to hurt.

Various strategies for managing investment pain may work well for one person and not for another. Here's my own plan for managing pain. I have two types of investments. The first is money that I don't expect I will ever need for myself or my family. This money is under my control, but I intend that someday it will go to my children. I'm not counting on departing this world any time soon, and I've allocated this money aggressively using active risk management and, in some cases, leverage. I'm shooting for an average annual total return of 20 to 25 percent. I think this is a reasonable goal for aggressive investors with a high tolerance for risk, and that's appropriate for this money.

My pain threshold for this money is a loss of 30 percent in one year. I want to make sure you understand that any loss at all will be painful to me, and a loss of 30 percent would be very uncomfortable. I am willing to continue these investments knowing that I could lose that much, though I think it's highly unlikely that will happen.

My other investments are for my immediate family and my own retirement. I know that I can reach my personal financial goals if I continue to earn at least 8 percent, compounded. My goal is to achieve a 12 percent return, giving me a substantial margin for error.

My pain tolerance for this money is more limited. I have what you could call a "bag lady" personality, worrying (not very rationally) that I might run out of money before I run out of life. With this retirement money, I am willing to accept no more than a 10 percent annual loss.

What happens if my losses exceed my thresholds? In either case, losses greater than my threshold would cause me to reevaluate my whole strategy. A loss outside my limits would indicate circumstances that had changed beyond what I understand now. And it would mean my carefully crafted strategies had become inadequate to deal with that new reality.

This would put me into unknown territory, and I don't know for certain how I would respond. I suspect one of my first responses would be to start saving more money each month to try to make up for the loss. And I certainly would consider taking a less aggressive investment posture in the future, perhaps putting more emphasis on bonds and less on equities.

I suggest you determine your own pain threshold. Reduce it to numbers if you can. This will require you to understand yourself, and that can be beneficial in itself. Remember, when you pass your pain threshold, your decisions will be less reliable and more risky. That's when you want to be able to take a written plan out of your desk drawer or file cabinet.

WATCH OUT FOR THE MEDIA

Anxiety, one of an investor's major enemies, is goaded by the media. The job of the media is not to look out for your interests and make you a better investor. Perhaps you think the folks at *Money Magazine* have done your homework for you. Unfortunately, that's not how it really works. In real life, the job of the media is to keep your attention for the benefit of advertisers. It's even worse than that. Many of the articles in financial publications were spawned in the public relations departments of mutual fund companies, brokerage houses, or other firms that make and sell financial products.

Media companies learned long ago that it's next to impossible to sell magazines, newspapers, or television shows unless they have something new, different, exciting, and better. Which would you pick up first—a magazine promising to tell you about a hot new investment or a magazine with a cover story saying a 25-year-old investment plan is still the best one?

Every hour, every day, every week, every month the media have to hawk something new and different. If you are persuaded to buy a fund or a stock this month, you've got to be tempted to do something else next month. Otherwise, you'll be just one less reader (or listener or viewer) who can be delivered to advertisers next month.

The media offer a parade of experts who slice and dice every part of the financial world before your eyes and ears, often 24 hours a day. And how useful are all these experts? Not very. For any financial topic you can think of, I could find at least two highly qualified experts who would take opposite positions on the meaning of any particular situation. The media like to quote these people's views as if they were facts instead of interpretations and guesses.

Some big brokerage houses employ people whose only job is to answer media questions about the pulse of the market. None of these people has any reliable way to know why the market is doing whatever it's doing. But does that stop them? Not a bit!

Consider the following imaginary dialogue, which could pass for wisdom and insight at any financial broadcasting concern:

Anchor: "John, why are investors reacting this way?"

Guest: "Well, Carol, I think people are nervous about what the Fed might do at its next meeting."

Anchor: "Thanks, John."

Thanks? Thanks for what? John's comment says absolutely nothing. Yet if it were on tape it could be dropped into any broadcast at any time on any day picked at random. And it would be absolutely right at home in the blather that makes up financial broadcast journalism.

I want to tell you a story about a client who couldn't separate his carefully plotted strategy from what was happening in the broader market.

After extensive discussions with this very smart client, we set up a worldwide balanced account for him with four equally weighted categories of assets: U.S. stocks, U.S. bonds, international stocks, and international bonds. We expected this mix would give him just the right combination of limited risk along with reasonable expected returns that would meet his needs. There was no question that he completely understood what we were doing.

About six months later, he called to say he was quite upset that his account was underperforming the Dow Jones Industrial Average, which had been doing quite well and which had been in the media spotlight. On a rational level, this client's complaint made no sense. Half his portfolio was in bonds, and only 12.5 percent was invested in large-cap U.S. stocks like the 30 that make up the Dow Jones index. There was no way his portfolio could mirror the Dow. What could he have been expecting?

When I reminded him that we purposely set up his account to make sure it did not match the Dow, he assured me he understood that on an intellectual level. But his anxiety was not based on reason. His emotional side told him that he had come to an investment professional for money management, and now he felt as if we were not on top of his account and the market.

His emotional reaction was akin to turning on your car radio when you are stopped cold on a freeway, and then getting angry when you hear that several other freeways are wide open. It's an understandable reaction, but not very rational and not very useful. We worked through this issue with him, and he stuck with his carefully crafted plan.

THE TWO LISTS

Many people think they have to figure out whether the market is too high or too low. But can they do it? Let me describe a mental exercise I do for fun every now and then, one I often present in the workshops I lead. I call it "the two lists."

The folks on Wall Street always have an "A" list of reasons the market is almost certainly going up and a "B" list of reasons it's almost certainly headed downward. Every item on each list is plausible and seems important. I usually believe everything on each one. The problem is that the A list is just as solid as the B list, and vice versa. All the changing and conflicting items on these lists give you no rational basis for making investment decisions

For example, here's an abbreviated version of the two lists that I compiled in 2004:

A. *Reasons the market will go up:* The long-time president of the Federal Reserve Bank of San Francisco recently predicted strong economic growth with little risk of inflation beyond 1.5 percent. Employment is rising. Corporations are leaner and meaner than they were a few years ago and are reporting higher profits. The Fed isn't expected to raise interest rates very fast. Many investors are still on the sidelines in the aftermath of the recent bear market. They are sitting on huge cash reserves that could go into the market at any time, driving up demand for stocks.

B. *Reasons the market will go down:* Wall Street thrives on certainty, which is a scarce commodity these days. Continuing violence in Iraq undermines confidence in global stability and commerce. There is no way to know how or when the United States will be able to disengage. Alan Greenspan has publicly stated what's been patently obvious for years: interest rates will have to go up. Inflationary pressures are heating up in Asia. Gasoline prices are at record levels. Corporate and mutual fund scandals have eroded investors' confidence.

Each of those lists could be expanded by a mile. If you had to choose one of them, how would you do it?

Unfortunately, many investors don't know what they believe and why they believe it. As a result, they adopt a view of the market based on who they heard when they happened to be in a receptive mood. For no reason I've ever understood, many people give particular credence to what they hear from somebody sitting next to them in an airplane. I hate to think how many people have a view of the market, and thus make major decisions that affect their financial future, based on somebody's personality or charm or the emotional content of a particular point of view.

THE ANSWER

The right way to deal with most broadcast financial journalism is to either change the station or turn off the radio or TV. The wrong way, as I stated in Chapter 1, is to make investment moves based on what you see or hear on these programs.

Here's the straight scoop: From time to time you will know exactly what you ought to do as an investor. And you simply won't want to do it. The most basic investment decision is the one you face when you have some money that you could either set aside or spend. Particularly if you have a family, there will be times when you'll want to spend that money instead of save it.

To invest money requires postponing gratification. This is an ability (or willingness) that signifies a level of maturity. If you can't learn to do that, you will never be much of an investor. If your savings plan depends on how you feel every time you get a paycheck, that plan doesn't have much of a chance.

Solution: Put your investments on automatic pilot. Have money deducted from your paycheck and deposited in a 401(k) account or automatically withdrawn from your bank account and put into a mutual fund's automatic investment plan. Make this decision once, not every time you get paid. Pay yourself first (before you spend any money) and pay yourself automatically.

There will be times when you'll want to follow some interesting tip or idea you hear about. Don't do it. To remove (or at least greatly reduce) temptation, make sure your new investments are automatically being allocated in the right way. There will be times when you won't want to go to the trouble of rebalancing. If you can, make this happen automatically once a year. Your best defense against your emotions and against the influences of Wall Street and the media is to get things figured out once, then let other people and their computers carry out your wishes. That will make your life a lot more pleasant. And it will certainly make you a better investor.

Part II

You Can Win the Retirement Game

Chapter FIVE

Who Are You and What Are Your Goals?

If you don't know who you are, the stock market is an
expensive place to find out.

—George Goodman

This book contains the information, insights, and directions
necessary for investors to thrive. But these tools won't help
you unless you apply them properly to your own circumstances. This chapter tells you how to do that by estimating
some important mileposts on your journey to financial independence. To make your money do more for you, it's first
necessary to answer the question "more of what?" This
question is trickier than you might think, because it depends
on the interplay of several important things that only you can
figure out.

To get a good handle on your own circumstances, the
most important figure is the income you will need the first

year you retire. The word "need" is critical. Your basic needs—food, clothing, shelter, and medical care—must be met no matter what. We call this figure your base target. You'll also want to compute a second target annual retirement income that would be enough to support your desires for such nonessential things as traveling, building or buying a second home, and leaving a substantial estate. We call this figure your live-it-up target, because it represents the grander life you want to live.

Once you have determined those two numbers, you can figure out how much retirement income must come from your investments to reach each of these targets. Then you can easily calculate a ballpark figure for how big your portfolio should be when you retire. If you're still working with 10 or more years to go before retirement, this ballpark figure is probably good enough to direct your investing for the time being. When you get close to retirement, you'll want to fine-tune the numbers and think seriously about how you'll withdraw the money. We take up that topic in Chapter 13.

Early in my retirement workshops, I ask for a show of hands in the audience to get people to start thinking about their primary investment goals. "How many of you want to beat the market?" Some hands always go up. "How many of you want to get the highest return you can get within your risk tolerance?" Lots of hands. "Who wants to find the lowest-risk way to meet your needs?" A few hands go up.

By this time, I can see a little uncertainty on people's faces. Each one of these goals seems pretty attractive, and often investors think they want to achieve them all. They want to beat the market; they want high returns; and they want low risks. Some people are primarily competitive. They'll most likely choose beating the market. Others are oriented toward return, while still others are oriented toward security and safety.

This much I know: You can't successfully pursue all three of these goals at once, at least not with the same pool of money. You've got to choose, and you should do it purposefully. If you don't have a focus, Wall Street will be happy to create one for you. It will invariably be whatever the investment industry has decided is the current path of least resistance to selling you something.

Almost all the advertisements for financial services stress beating the market. They may call it doing better or getting performance. But I don't think you'll find many ads that promote being like the crowd. However, as we saw in Chapter 4, beating the market isn't all it's cracked up to be.

Most of the participants in my workshops have their hearts set on getting the highest returns they can. And what could be wrong with that? Nothing, actually, except that you might not make it. If all you want is the highest possible return, watch the big billboards for the national Mega-Lottery. When the jackpot gets up over $200 million, "invest" your money in tickets. The payoff will be so high that no financial calculator will be able to compute your percentage return. You say that's not exactly what you had in mind? Oh! That's why I tell people to never, ever say you're looking for the highest possible return without adding "within my risk tolerance."

The third possible objective, finding the lowest-risk way to meet your needs, is very attractive. I wish it were easier to accomplish. It's easier (and more pleasant) to figure out the return that you want than it is to determine how much risk you can take. The first is a function of mathematics, the second a function of emotions. But it's equally valuable to know your risk tolerance, because it's easier to do something about it.

For example, if you tell me you can tolerate no more than a 15 percent one-year loss, it's relatively easy for me to "dial in" a mix of investments with enough risk that you're likely to lose 15 percent in some future 12-month period. A loss like that is a one-time event, and it's easy to tell whether or not it occurred.

On the other hand, if you tell me you need an annualized return of 10 percent over 20 or 30 years, I can suggest investments that have achieved that long-term return in the past. But your objective is a long-term cumulative result, and it could take decades before you will know for sure whether or not you succeeded.

On your way to the long-term future, you must get through the short-term future. In the first 12 months after you begin an investment plan, your return could be a gain of 30 percent or a loss of 15 percent. You won't complain about the gain, but how can I show you that your 15-percent loss is part of a long-term annualized 10 percent return? I can't!

The upshot is that I recommend you do your best to estimate both your need for return and your tolerance for risk. We'll focus on risk tolerance in Chapter 10, where you'll learn exactly how to find an investment mix that will come close to meeting your needs for safety and for return. In this chapter, we'll look at how to determine how much money you need in order to retire. That way you will know what you must do between now and then.

In my workshop, I ask people what annual return they want. I give them a range of choices, from under 8 percent all the way up to 15 percent and above. Not surprisingly, participants typically prefer higher returns to lower ones. I then ask them what return they need. Most don't know. Because this second number is critical, I want to walk you through the drill to figure it out. This exercise will give you only a ballpark figure at best. But unless you are on the brink of retirement or already retired, this ballpark figure may be sufficient to direct your course. As you get closer to retirement, you should run the exercise again, perhaps once a year, striving for increasing accuracy. The better the numbers you put into this, the more valuable your results will be.

Your first task is to determine how much money you will need to live on during retirement. This is your base target. You want to find a figure that will cover your essential needs for food, clothing, shelter, and health care. Include your utilities and personal care and enough for a modest level of gifts, entertainment, and hobbies. Don't forget taxes.

You should be able to get a rough estimate of your needs from your current spending, with some modifications. [After you're retired, you won't need to keep contributing to an IRA or a 401(k) plan. But you probably will pay more for medical care— possibly a lot more.]

The result will be an income estimate that could sustain you in retirement but not give you all the choices you'd like to have. Use today's dollars, without regard to inflation, an issue we'll address momentarily. This number is your base target.

Your second task is to estimate your live-it-up target. Start with the base target and add money for the optional but desirable things you want to do and have in retirement. These are discretionary expenses that you can cut if necessary. Travel, a second home, hobbies, and other activities are all part of this calculation.

How much desired income you add is totally subjective and up to you. Shoot for a level that seems very attractive, but not necessarily extravagant. For most people, a retirement income of $1 million a year (at least in today's dollars) is unrealistic and won't ever happen. You might like that idea, but that number won't be useful. If your live-it-up target is 1.5 to 2 times the size of your basic target, you're probably within the range of reality.

Here's how you'll use these two figures:

Your base target will determine whether and when you can afford to retire. Until you have enough assets (along with other sources of income) to give you this income, you'll need to keep accumulating savings. Your live-it-up target will tell you when it might be time to declare that "enough is enough." If your assets are sufficient to achieve this level of income, you're in good shape to live the life to which you aspire. You can keep working past that point, of course, but you won't have to continue to save so aggressively. However, you will probably need to continue adding to your savings until the day you retire. The reason? Inflation.

We'll deal with inflation again in Chapter 13. Here, we're trying to get you into the ballpark. While you're accumulating assets, the way to account for inflation is to update your base target and your live-it-up target figures once a year. As you do that, you'll automatically adjust for higher prices for the things you spend money on. For example, if your overall expenses go up 5 percent, that will boost your base target. And as we're about to see, that will automatically adjust the size of the portfolio you need.

To illustrate this next step, let's pick a couple of figures out of the blue and work with them. Assume you have determined that if you were to retire today, your base target is $60,000 and that you desire a lifestyle that could be supported on $100,000 a year (your live-it-up target). This means that $60,000 becomes the all-important number.

The chances are excellent that you won't have to rely on your portfolio for the whole $60,000. You'll probably have Social Security; you may have a pension; and you might have other sources of income you can rely on such as annuity payments or rental income from real estate. You should have an individual benefits estimate from the Social Security Administration that is no more than a year old which gives you a pretty good idea what to expect. If you aren't sure you trust Social Security and you want to be conservative, reduce that estimate by some percentage so you won't count on it.

Add up all that nonportfolio expected income and convert it to an annual figure. In our example, let's assume all those payments add up to $25,000 a year. That leaves you with a "gap" of $35,000 that must come from your portfolio every year to meet your $60,000 base target. The $100,000 live-it-up target leaves a gap of $75,000 to come from your portfolio.

At this point you can start to get a good handle on your retirement picture. You can see that your portfolio will have to provide at least $35,000 a year of sustainable income, and that it would be nice to have $75,000. If you can save enough to fall between those numbers, you will be in the ballpark.

A quick-and-dirty rule of thumb is to multiply that yearly gap by 20. The result tells you how big your portfolio should be on the day you retire. That implies that you will withdraw 5 percent of the portfolio for your first year. (As we will see in Chapter 13, a carefully designed portfolio can likely sustain that withdrawal rate for the rest of your life, although there are no guarantees.)

In this example, that means your portfolio, if you were going to retire today, should be at least $700,000 (20 times $35,000). Ideally, it would be worth $1.5 million (20 times $75,000). With this calculation, suddenly your situation snaps into sharper focus. If you currently have $1 million, you know that you're on track. If you're only a few years away from your expected retirement date and your resources fall far short, you may have to work longer, increase your savings, or change your expectations for retirement—or some combination of all three. If this is the case, the sooner you find out about it, the more you can do about it.

Using a financial calculator or the help of an adviser, you can use this information to plan your savings rate or calculate the time you'll be able to retire. For example, if you have accumulated $600,000 and you want to retire in two years, you'll need to contribute aggressively in order to have a high probability of beating your $700,000 base target by much.

For another example, if you have $400,000 and you're adding $12,000 a year, a financial calculator can tell you that steady annual returns of 10 percent will take you to $700,000 in a bit under five years. Knowing that future market returns are uncertain and that your living costs will probably go up (meaning you'll need more than $700,000 to retire), you might use that information to target a retirement date in eight years. With 10 percent returns, that would give you $994,666 on retirement day. Using the 5 percent rule, that would provide a first-year retirement withdrawal of just under $50,000. If these calculations indicate a serious gap between what you can save and what you'll need, that's a strong indication that you could benefit from some professional help. (In Chapter 15, we'll discuss how to find such help.)

Here are a few other things to keep in mind as you do your calculations:

Try to avoid the common mistake of overestimating your

expected investment return. You'll probably want to become more conservative as you get closer to retirement, blending more fixed-income funds with your equity funds. That will give you stability, but it will most likely also you a lower return.

Emergencies and unwelcome life changes occur, often with significant expenses attached. When you're working, you can often recover from these things by redirecting your income, taking a second job, cutting back expenses, or even (although of course I don't recommend it) by reducing your savings for awhile. But when you're retired, emergencies can turn into serious financial setbacks. Think about how you will deal with the risks of disability, death of a spouse or partner (which could reduce pension income), long-term care, and helping aging parents.

You can transfer some of those risks by buying insurance (and the premiums must become part of your budget). But the best plan may be a separate emergency fund. Therefore, consider whether you should increase the multiplier we used above (20 times your first-year retirement income) to 21 or 22.

You might want to add yet another digit or two to the multiplier, depending on what your first-year retirement plans are. The first year of retirement is when many people have large one-time expenses such as buying a motor home or taking off for an extended trip to Europe. You'll need to make sure you can adequately fund any such first-year plans that you have. Be sure to discuss these issues with your spouse or partner, because both of you will be affected by the plans and choices you make. This is also a worthwhile topic to discuss with a financial planner, to make sure your plans and expectations are realistic.

I don't recommend shortcuts for estimating your expenses in retirement, but I know that many people take them. If you use your current income as the source for your base target, be wary of any formula that assumes you will need less money after you retire than before. That's not what usually happens.

Finally, you should figure out how you will measure your investment progress. In our society of conspicuous consumption, you may compare yourself (and your status in life) to your neighbors or your peers. If the neighbors have a new car or a new boat, should you have one too? The trouble is, your neighbors may be living the high life on borrowed money, building up a pile of debt that will come back to haunt them later. You probably don't know. Your neighbor may have inherited $800,000 and thus be able to afford lots of spending that you can't. You probably don't know.

Your neighbors' investment results are an equally lousy benchmark for you—even if you had that information. Your neighbor is unlikely to produce brokerage and mutual fund statements for you to look at. You'll be more likely to hear about the successes than the setbacks, and thus (assuming you care), you'll get an inaccurate picture of what is going on next door.

As we saw in Chapter 4, "the market" is a lousy benchmark that could require you to whine about very positive returns and brag about losing substantial amounts of money. In the end, the only benchmark that really matters is one you can now create for yourself: how you're doing in terms of meeting your own goals and needs.

If you follow the steps outlined in this chapter and repeat the analysis once a year so, and you adjust your base target and your live-it-up target accordingly, you'll be miles ahead of most investors. And you'll be ready to apply what you will learn in the next five chapters of this book: how to make your money do the most for you.

Chapter SIX

Your Perfect Portfolio

███████

A workman who wants to do his work well must first sharpen his tools.

—*Confucius*

Investors willing to give up chasing recent performance and trying to pick tomorrow's hottest managers can fall back on nearly 80 years of performance data. In this chapter we show how those data can be used to put together a world-class portfolio of low-cost mutual funds investing in asset classes that are likely to continue to outperform the Standard & Poor's 500 Index.

We recommend an investment program that is boringly predictable instead of dazzling and exciting. We call it "Your Perfect Portfolio," and we'll show you in this and the following chapters how to put it together. The goal, in a nutshell, is to give investors a piece of the action along with peace of mind. What investors need most is a strategy with enough power in good times to generate positive returns, coupled with enough protection in bad times to keep those investors from bailing out in discouragement.

This chapter looks in detail at the nature of diversification, noting the difference between real diversification and mere window-dressing. The latter, unfortunately, is much too common in 401(k) plans and the offerings of mutual fund companies.

As a point of reference, we look at how the pension funds of large U.S. companies have traditionally invested most of their money. We measure this model in terms of its risk and returns. This model is typically allocated 60 percent to stocks and 40 percent to bonds. Its returns are strong enough, and its risks tame enough, that it could meet the long-term needs of most investors. We see that the pension funds' strategy can be approximated using only two index funds.

Any investment strategy worthy of being called "perfect" must be held to a high standard. For our purposes, that means our goal is a plan that will provide higher returns and lower risks than the pension fund model, using no-load funds readily available to ordinary investors.

The key to making this work is smart equity diversification. The portfolio includes value stocks as well as growth stocks, small-cap stocks as well as large-cap stocks, and international stocks in addition to U.S. stocks.

Your Perfect Portfolio will combine multiple asset classes, every one of which has higher risk than the S&P 500 Index. Yet when you combine them properly, their individual risks offset each other and produce a lower composite risk figure. The construction of Your Perfect Portfolio starts with an examination of the 40 percent fixed-income component in typical pension funds. Standard practice is to invest in long-term and intermediate-term bonds. But we show that investors can get nearly all the return of those bonds, at less risk, by investing in shorter-term bonds.

By the end of the chapter we will have built the foundation for putting together Your Perfect Portfolio.

With his permission, I want to begin this chapter by drawing on some of the work of my son, Jeff Merriman-Cohen. He wrote an article that's available on the web site for this book. It's called "The Perfect Portfolio," and it reflects the process we often go through with new clients.

Risk, as we saw in earlier chapters, is central to investing. In a bond, there are two main risks: maturity and credit. Maturity refers to the fact that rising interest rates tend to depress the prices of longer-term bonds more than shorter-term bonds. This makes long-term bonds riskier than short-term bonds. Credit risk refers to the fact that repayment is more reliable from a blue chip company than from one that's struggling to meet its obligations.

In any particular stock, there are many risks. But in the aggregate, as Jeff wrote so succinctly, stocks are more risky than bonds, smaller companies are more risky than large ones, and "value" companies are riskier than growth companies. These risks are well known, and over long periods of time value stocks and small company stocks have offered investors higher returns than growth stocks and large company stocks.

From 1927 through 2004, U.S. small-cap value stocks as a group (meaning all such stocks, not just a selection of them) produced an annualized return of 14.8 percent—or 4.4 percentage points above that of the S&P 500 Index. This asset class experienced a 12-year period, from 1975 through 1986, with no annual losses and cumulative gains of 2,148 percent, or about 29.6 percent annualized. Astonishing!

However, small-cap value stocks had 22 negative years from 1927 through 2002. Those losses averaged 18.3 percent. The biggest annual loss was 53.5 percent, part of a four-year losing streak with cumulative losses of about 85 percent. (That four-year streak, by the way, was immediately followed by a one-year gain of 142.5 percent. That looks mighty good on paper, but if you're down to 15 cents on the dollar of your original investment, a 142.5 percent gain brings you back up to only 36 cents.)

I'll discuss small-cap stocks and value stocks in later chapters. The question here is how investors can take advantage of asset classes like that without getting bruised and burned.

How Reliable Are Stocks?

It's easy to see that stocks are more risky than fixed-income investments, and that much of the time they provide higher returns. But just how reliable is this premium return? And how long must an investor wait to be sure of getting it? Those are excellent questions. Investors who know the answers will have a real advantage over those who don't.

Investors have every reason to expect that stock investments will continue to provide premium returns over the long term. But over shorter periods, this won't always be the case. You should expect to see occasional multiyear periods when cash outperforms stocks (think of 2000 through 2002).

A study that included thousands of computer trials using actual market data from 1926 through 2004 gives some useful insight on the size and reliability of the equity market premium. The study, summarized in Table 6.1, compares the returns of the S&P 500 Index to that of no-risk Treasury bills.

To understand the table, start in the "1 year" column. The figures were derived from studying every possible 12-month period (for example February 1967 through January 1968) from 1926 through 2004.

The numbers in the "best," "average," and "worst" boxes are differences of return, expressed in percentage points. Here's how they work: In these 937 one-year periods, the average return from stocks was 8.9 percentage points higher than the corresponding return from T-bills. That means that if T-bills returned 5 percent, stocks returned 13.9 percent.

In the very best one-year period, if T-bills returned 5 percent, stocks returned 168 percent. In the worst period, stocks suffered a very sharp loss, equal to 68.9 percentage points below the return of T-bills.

The most important number is the bottom one, "reliability." It indicates that in any 12 consecutive months, investors in equities had about two chances out of three of exceeding the return of T-bills. The other columns in the table show that the reliability factor increased until it reached 100 percent in periods of 20 years and longer. You'll also see that the average premium increased rapidly with time.

Table 6.1

Equity Premiums, 1926–2004

Period	1 year	5 years	10 years	15 years	20 years	25 years
Best	163	366	578	1,246	2,486	4,814
Average	8.9	54.3	168	390	783	1,363
Worst	−68.9	−76.1	−64.2	−76.7	16	191
Reliability	67.8%	77.8%	85.5%	94.3%	100.0%	100.0%

The answer is smart diversification. When we meet with a client, we pull out the chart that you see as Figure 6.1. It's called the Theoretical Balance of Risk and Return (1973–2004). The graph looks very simple: a straight line! But in order to follow the upcoming discussion, you'll need to understand this graph.

This graph plots annual returns (in percentages, on the left) and levels of risk (in worst 12-month losses, along the bottom). Every point inside the graph represents a combination of a return and a level of risk. The area on the right side of the graph represents higher risks; the area on the left represents lower risks. Similarly, the area near the top represents higher returns, the area near the bottom lower returns. The ideal investment would be close to the upper left-hand corner of the graph, where risk is lowest and return is highest. We'll look at a series of graphs laid out this same way, always looking for combinations of assets that have more return and less risk.

In Figure 6.1, the top (right) end of the dotted line shows the

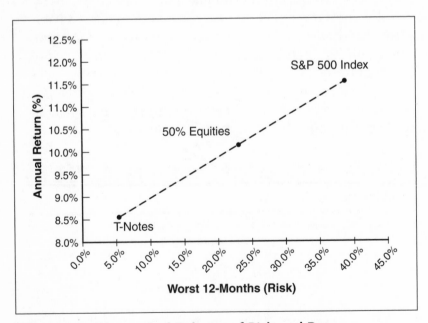

Figure 6.1   Theoretical Balance of Risk and Return (1970–2004)

risk and return of the S&P 500 Index from 1973 through 2004. The bottom (left) end of the line shows the risk and return of T-notes. Just as you would expect, T-notes have much less risk (and less return) than the S&P 500 Index. The point in the middle of the line shows what you might logically expect from a 50/50 combination of T-notes and the S&P 500 Index. This is the halfway point of both risk and return.

But in real life, it doesn't work out that way. You'll see that in Figure 6.2 [Actual Balance of Risk and Return (1973–2004)], which shows a solid line based on actual combinations of these two assets.

The solid line is bent upward and toward the left. You can see that the actual 50/50 combination produced a higher return than the average of the two individual returns, and at less risk.

Figure 6.3 adds some important information, showing where various percentage combinations of these two assets fall on this line. Every combination is higher than—and to the left of—where it would fall on the straight dotted line that we saw in

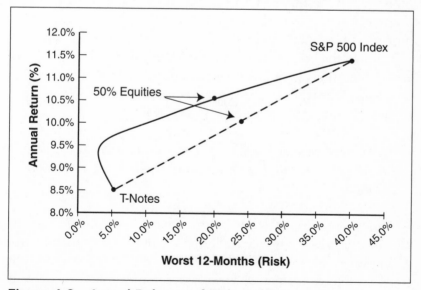

Figure 6.2   Actual Balance of Risk and Return (1970–2004)

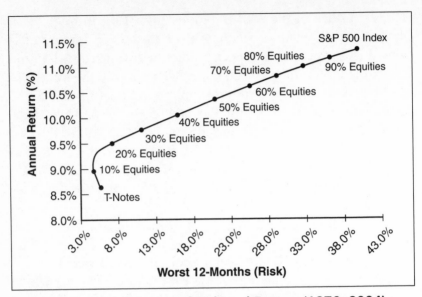

Figure 6.3   The Balance of Risk and Return (1970–2004)

Figure 6.1. One thing that pops out at me when I look at this graph is that the 20 percent equity combination has a 10 percent higher return than T-notes alone—with minimal additional risk.

Think of the bend in that line as a benefit of diversification. As we will see, this phenomenon is not limited to these two particular assets. In fact, these three graphs show something very fundamental that savvy investors should understand:

Smart diversification lets you mix two assets together and achieve a higher return, with less risk, than the average return of those two assets.

Choosing the right assets for this smart diversification is crucial, and in later chapters we'll discuss the most valuable ones and how to capture the premium returns they offer. But for right now, let's look further at "smart diversification" and why it works. Start with Figure 6.4 (Which Investment Would You Prefer?). This shows a theoretical graph of return over some period

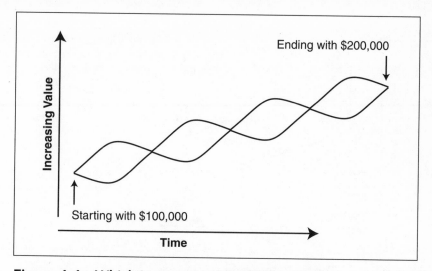

Figure 6.4   Which Investment Would You Prefer?

of time of two investments, each of which starts with $100,000 and winds up being worth $200,000. Which one do you think is better?

Many of our clients have a tough time choosing between these, and for good reason. They are mirror images of each other, and they wind up in the same place. (The only significant difference between them is that the investment that initially rises is less risky, in hindsight, than the one that initially falls, for the obvious reason that the former is never worth less than its initial cost.)

Instead of requiring clients to pick one of these, we turn their attention to a graph called "Perfect Diversification," which you will see in Figure 6.5. The straight line up the middle represents the progress of a 50/50 combination of the two investments shown in Figure 6.4.

These two theoretical assets have identical long-term rates of return. But in the shorter term, they are 100 percent negatively correlated: each one does the exact opposite of the other.

This is critical: Individually, each of these assets produces a good deal of angst in getting to its final result. But when they are

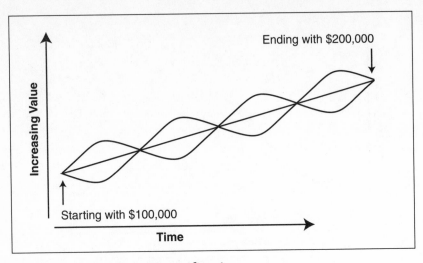

Figure 6.5   Perfect Diversification

put together, they achieve the same result with no angst at all. This is the key to making your money work hard for you while staying within your risk tolerance. Perfect diversification like this doesn't happen in real life, but it's a worthwhile goal to have a pool of investments that go steadily upward. For diversification to work, it has to involve more than just owning different assets. They have to be assets that behave differently from each other.

This is why it doesn't do investors much good to hold several funds that behave similarly to the S&P 500 Index. Doing so may feel comfortable. But as one of my colleagues likes to say, three boxes of different brands of corn flakes may look different on the shelf, but what you get in the end is still just corn flakes.

The "just corn flakes" problem is more common than you might think. It turns out that many institutional investors fall into the same traps as individuals. Lots of 401(k) plans have multiple options that overlap each other and are focused mostly on large-cap U.S. stocks. It's not uncommon to find 401(k) plans that offer half a dozen such funds and perhaps a mid-cap stock fund but nothing at all in the way of small-cap funds. And we've seen

401(k) plans that don't offer any value funds or international funds. That's a real disservice to plan participants, as we will see later in this book.

For now, let's concentrate on the fixed-income component of the typical pension fund portfolio. This makes up 40 percent of our perfect portfolio, and it's surprisingly easy to get it right. Whether your portfolio is heavy on bonds or light on bonds, it matters what kind of bonds you put into the mix. In general, longer bond maturities have higher risks and higher yields, and vice versa. You can see this relationship in Figure 6.6 (Risk/Reward: Does It Pay to Extend Maturities?).

The bottom line in the chart measures risk; the top one measures compound return. The critical point is where those lines cross: at maturities of about five years. The chart shows that bonds with maturities above five years are consistently more risky, but not consistently more rewarding. The longest maturity you needed in this period (and we don't have any reason to think the future will be substantially different) to achieve high bond returns was five years.

And in fact, one-year T-bills provided about 90 percent of the return of the five-year notes, with much less volatility. In the accounts we manage for clients in which bonds are used to stabilize a portfolio that also includes equities, we use a 50/50 combination of two fixed-income funds, one with maturities of up to two years and the other with maturities of up to five years. Individual investors can achieve a close approximation of this with a typical short-term bond fund. This is a simple but effective way to begin building Your Perfect Portfolio.

You'll see this in Figures 6.7 and 6.8. The first one shows Portfolio 1, the standard pension fund portfolio, with a bond component that has an average maturity of 10 to 13 years. You'll see the portfolio's annualized return (10.4 percent) and its annualized standard deviation, a common measure of risk.

In Figure 6.8 you see the effect of replacing the longer-term bond index with a shorter-term fixed-income component. The result is Portfolio 2, which has a slightly higher return (10.6 per-

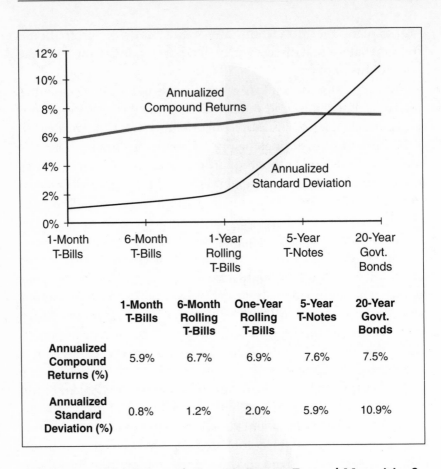

**Figure 6.6   Risk/Reward: Does It Pay to Extend Maturities?
(January 1964–December 2004)**

	1-Month T-Bills	6-Month Rolling T-Bills	One-Year Rolling T-Bills	5-Year T-Notes	20-Year Govt. Bonds
Annualized Compound Returns (%)	5.9%	6.7%	6.9%	7.6%	7.5%
Annualized Standard Deviation (%)	0.8%	1.2%	2.0%	5.9%	10.9%

cent) along with more stability, a standard deviation that fell by almost one percentage point.

This is only the first step in creating the ideal combination of assets to let you retire in style. But even if you stopped here, this change would provide a smoother ride along the way. The move to short-term bonds gives more of what you want from bonds—stability. And it doesn't extract a severe price in performance.

The best is yet to come.

Figure 6.7   Portfolio 1

Figure 6.8   Portfolio 2

Chapter SEVEN

Why Size Really Does Matter

███████

Tall oaks from little acorns grow.

—David Everett

If you want your retirement savings to work hard for you, there are three main changes you must make in the equity part of the standard pension fund's portfolio. One is to expand the asset mix to include stocks of smaller companies. Another is to include "value" companies that are out of favor. The third is to include international companies, ones headquartered outside the United States.

This chapter explores why small companies have historically produced bigger returns and how you can easily and efficiently capture them. The size effect is primarily a matter of potential. Investors looking for growth need to put their money where the growth potential lies, and one of those places is small companies. (Who's likely to grow more over the next year—a 13-year-old boy or a 27-year-old man?)

Compare two well-known companies with leading positions in important industries in the 1990s: IBM and Microsoft Corp. IBM sales grew from $69 billion in 1990 to $88 billion in 2000, a gain of 28 percent. Microsoft sales grew from $1.15 billion in 1990 to $23 billion in 2000, a gain of 1,896 percent. Shareholders who took the safer bet (in 1990) with IBM did well; that company's shares appreciated approximately 273 percent from mid-1990 to mid-2000. Microsoft, much smaller but hardly unknown in 1990, rewarded its shareholders with a gain of 3,689 percent in the same 10-year period. (Stock prices, supplied by Bloomberg L.P. and adjusted for splits, were measured from June 29, 1990 through June 30, 2000.)

The prudent way to benefit from small company returns is not to invest in individual stocks but in small company stocks as an asset class. (These are also known as small-cap stocks because the size of companies for this purpose is based on total market capitalization, the current stock price times the number of shares outstanding.) These returns can best be captured through mutual funds that invest in the whole asset class, not just a few small-cap stocks. Index funds are the most efficient vehicle for this.

Over long periods of time, small-cap stocks have outperformed large-cap ones. I expect this premium return to continue over the long haul. But in this case, "long" can really mean long. The effect can take decades to pay off, although investors whose timing is lucky can sometimes experience these gains quickly.

There are significant periods when small-cap stocks outperform, and vice versa. From 1994 through 2000, the largest U.S. stocks (large-cap) more than tripled in value, while the smallest 10 percent of stocks appreciated only about 80 percent. From 1975 through 1983, the largest 10 percent of U.S. stocks appreciated about 200 percent, while the smallest 10 percent gained about 1,300 percent. A series of dramatic charts in this chapter shows that size really does matter. The superior performance of small-cap stocks seems to persist in trends that last at least a few years. The same is true of large-cap stocks. But the charts also show that dramatic reversals can occur every few years, so it's not a good idea to invest exclusively in large-cap stocks or only in small-cap stocks.

There is no predictable pattern of how long these trends will last. In the seven time periods covered by our charts, small-cap stocks were king for periods of four to nine years. Large-cap stocks outperformed in periods that lasted from five to seven years.

As this is being written, small-cap stocks have been outperforming for several years. But investors shouldn't get suckered into thinking that whichever trend is current is "normal" and will continue indefinitely. Instead, they should own both large-cap stocks and small-cap stocks in roughly equal amounts. And they should maintain this balance by annual rebalancing.

Splitting the equity part of the standard pension fund portfolio between large-cap and small-cap stocks significantly improves the long-term return of that portfolio. This layer of diversification also reduces volatility.

Since the main thesis of this chapter is that size matters, let's move right to the "good stuff," by which I mean the evidence contained in half a dozen charts. These charts, which we have reprinted with permission from Dimensional Fund Advisors, cover the years 1965 through 2004, a 39-year period that's long enough to show you what you need to know about small and large companies.

Figure 7.1 shows the four years from 1965 through 1968, a period when small-cap stocks reigned supreme. The left-hand scale shows total return over this period. The bottom scale has 11 positions, 10 of which represent the U.S. stock market as if it were sliced into 10 "deciles."

To understand these, imagine that you had a list of all publicly traded stocks ranked by market capitalization (current stock price times outstanding shares). The 10 percent of names at the bottom of your list represent the tenth decile, the smallest U.S. companies you can invest in. The next 10 percent of names represents the ninth decile, and so forth, with the first decile representing the very largest companies.

The 11th position represents the S&P 500 Index, which is dominated by large, familiar U.S. companies like Wells Fargo, Proctor & Gamble, Wal-Mart, Pfizer, Citigroup, and Cisco. Each of these, by the way, was once a small company going through rapid growth that paid off in a big way for early investors.

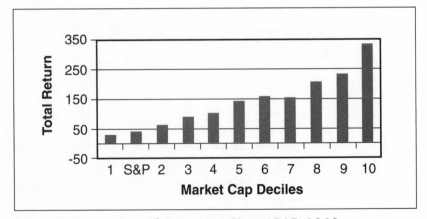

Figure 7.1   Impact of Company Size, 1965–1968

Figure 7.1 makes it clear that the size effect—smaller companies outperforming larger ones—apparently isn't random. All the way up and down that scale, smaller companies do better.

Figure 7.2, covering a period when stocks were declining, shows a strong reversal. In those years, the largest companies held up much better. Again, the size effect is unmistakable. Another reversal occurred in 1975, and small company stocks once again took over the leadership for nine years, as you can see in Figure 7.3.

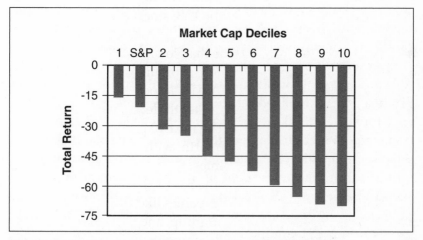

Figure 7.2   Impact of Company Size, 1969–1974

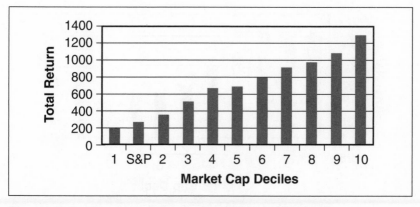

Figure 7.3   Impact of Company Size, 1975–1983

By the early 1980s, many investors had "learned" that small-cap companies were the ones that paid off. Imagine their surprise from 1984 through 1990, when (as you can see in Figure 7.4) large-cap stocks dwarfed the returns of small ones. The three-year period from 1991 through 1993 (Figure 7.5) indicates another reversal, followed by the five years shown in Figure 7.6, when large-cap stocks led the way once again. Figure 7.7 shows still another period of small-cap supremacy from 1999 through 2003.

It's not hard to see that over periods of several years or more, small-cap stocks and large-cap stocks go sharply in and out of favor among investors. Rarely have both groups been extremely productive or extremely unproductive at the same time.

Over much longer periods, small-cap stocks have shown a distinct advantage. From 1926 through 2004, small-cap U.S. stocks produced an annualized return of 13.1 percent, versus 10.4 percent for the S&P 500 Index. That difference of 2.7 percentage points might seem trivial, but it's not. Over a period of 40 years, which is well within the potential investment lifetime of most investors, an initial investment of $10,000 compounding at 10.4 percent (large-cap U.S. stocks) grows to $523,315. But if it compounded at 13.1 percent over 40 years, the same $10,000 would grow to almost $1.4 million.

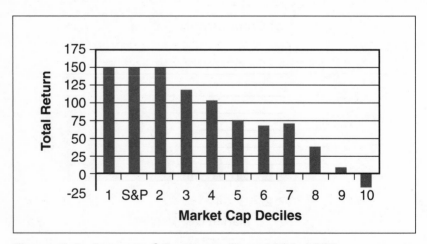

Figure 7.4   Impact of Company Size, 1984–1990

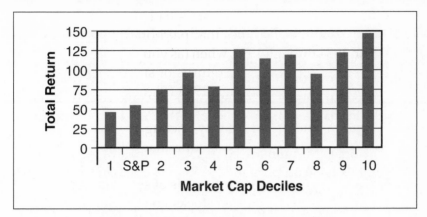

Figure 7.5   Impact of Company Size, 1991–1993

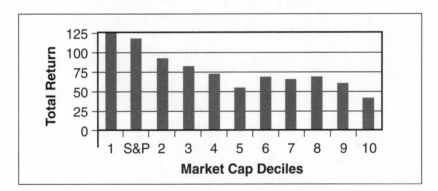

Figure 7.6   Impact of Company Size, 1994–1998

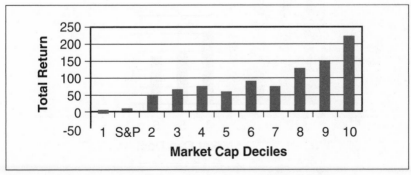

Figure 7.7   Impact of Company Size, 1999–2004

How Reliable Is the Premium from Small-Cap Stocks?

A study of 79 years of market history shows that the premium return from owing stocks of small-cap companies (as opposed to large-cap companies) is considerably more likely to manifest itself over long periods than in shorter ones.

The data are summarized in Table 7.1 below, identical in format to Table 6.1 presented (and explained) in Chapter 6. This table shows that in periods of 12 months, small-cap stocks had an average advantage of 7.1 percentage points over large-cap stocks. But as the bottom figure in the "1 year" column shows, only about 53 percent of the periods gave investors any premium return for investing in small-cap stocks. This premium became more reliable in periods lasting 10 years or more.

However, the figures also indicate that investors who rely totally on small-cap stocks could fall significantly behind even in a 25-year period. This is why we recommend that investors include large-cap stocks in their portfolios as well as small-cap stocks.

Table 7.1

Small-Cap Equity Premiums, 1926–2004

Period	1 year	5 years	10 years	15 years	20 years	25 years
Best	395	1,296	1,047	4,800	9,337	19,961
Average	7.1	53	118	329	796	1,917
Worst	–62.5	–149.1	–263	–791	–1,149	–452
Reliability	53.5%	55.5%	66.0%	73.5%	80.4%	92.4%

Small-cap investing works internationally, too, although reliable data aren't available for years before 1970. From 1970 through 2004, small-cap international companies compounded at 16.4 percent. That compares with 10.4 percent for large-cap international companies.

In Table 7.2, you'll find year-by-year results for small-cap U.S. stocks (compared with the S&P 500 Index) and small-cap international stocks (compared with the Morgan Stanley Europe Australia Far East Index known as EAFE).

Table 7.2

Small-Cap versus Large-Cap Stocks, U.S. and International

Year	U.S. large	U.S. small	Int. large	Int. small	Combined
1970	4.0	−16.7	−11.7	0.9	−5.9
1971	14.3	18.1	29.6	68.3	32.6
1972	19.0	−1.0	36.4	64.2	29.6
1973	−14.7	−40.7	−14.9	−13.7	−21.0
1974	−26.5	−29.3	−23.2	−28.6	−26.9
1975	37.2	69.9	35.4	49.9	48.1
1976	23.8	54.5	2.5	11.5	23.1
1977	−7.2	22.1	18.0	74.1	26.8
1978	6.6	21.8	32.6	65.5	31.6
1979	18.4	44.2	4.8	−0.8	16.7
1980	32.4	34.7	22.6	35.5	31.3
1981	−4.9	7.8	−2.3	−4.7	−1.0
1982	21.4	27.6	−1.9	0.8	12.0
1983	22.5	39.7	23.7	32.4	29.6
1984	6.3	−6.7	7.4	10.1	4.3
1985	32.2	24.7	56.2	60.1	43.3
1986	18.5	6.9	69.4	50.1	36.2
1987	5.2	−9.3	24.6	70.6	22.8
1988	16.8	22.9	28.3	26.0	23.5
1989	31.5	10.2	10.5	29.3	20.4
1990	−3.2	−21.6	−23.4	−16.8	−16.2

(continues)

Table 7.2 (continued)

Year	U.S. large	U.S. small	Int. large	Int. small	Combined
1991	30.1	44.6	15.9	7.1	24.4
1992	7.3	23.3	−13.1	−18.4	−0.2
1993	9.6	21.0	25.9	33.5	22.5
1994	1.3	3.1	5.3	12.4	5.5
1995	37.1	34.5	13.0	0.5	21.3
1996	22.6	17.6	6.3	2.6	12.3
1997	33.1	22.8	5.5	−23.7	9.4
1998	28.7	−7.3	18.2	8.2	11.9
1999	20.8	29.8	28.5	21.9	25.2
2000	−9.3	−3.6	−14.0	−5.4	−8.1
2001	−12.1	22.8	−20.8	−10.5	−5.2
2002	−22.2	−13.3	−14.6	1.9	−12.0
2003	28.5	60.7	36.7	58.8	46.2
2004	10.7	18.4	18.8	30.9	19.7
Compound Rate of Return	11.2	13.0	10.4	16.5	13.4
Growth of $10,000	$410,151	$723,909	$315,454	$2,109,638	$817,995
Standard deviation	17.4	26.5	18.5	20.9	16.9
Worst month	−21.5	−29.2	−14.5	−12.6	−18.8
Worst 3 months	−29.5	−32.6	−21.3	−24.2	−21.8
Worst 12 months	−38.9	−40.7	−38.2	−41.3	−38.7
Worst 36 months	−41.2	−58.5	−46.1	−27.3	−31.1
Worst 60 months	−18.0	−59.1	−28.2	−19.6	−9.6

At the bottom of each column are three cumulative figures that apply to the whole period: compound rate of return (CRR); the results of an initial $10,000 left to grow; and standard deviation, a measure of risk. (The most important thing to know about standard deviation is that smaller numbers indicate less risk.)

Small-cap investing has been productive. But it hasn't been easy. In the extended periods when small-cap stocks fall behind larger ones, investors can easily lose faith. That's why it's useful to remember why small-cap stocks tend to outperform over long periods. In general, investors get paid for taking risks, especially for taking prudent risks. As you can see from the standard deviation line in Table 7.2, small-cap stocks can be riskier than large-cap ones, although in this period the standard deviation was slightly less with small international stocks than with large international ones.

Small-cap stocks are riskier because they are newer companies, typically with fewer products, less depth of management, and higher costs of capital. And of course they don't have long, reassuring track records. They are the Yahoos and the Amazon.coms of the world rather than the IBMs and the General Electrics.

A large, mature company has already proven it can survive competition and weather economic storms. An upstart can fall on its face, and many do. Smaller companies can produce better returns because they can grow faster. I don't see any reason to think this basic relationship will change. I believe small companies will continue to be riskier than large ones. I believe that over time investors in small companies will continue to be rewarded for taking those higher risks. But over shorter periods, I believe small-cap investing will continue to be challenging because of periods like those shown in Figures 7.2, 7.4, and 7.6, when large-cap stocks did much better than small-cap ones.

The answer is to invest in both small-cap and large-cap stocks—and to rebalance every year. This annual rebalancing keeps the risk of this combination in check. And it forces you to take some profits each year from whichever size category, large or small, has outperformed and then put those profits into the underperforming category. (Hint: This is called buying low and selling high. It's something that successful investors do.)

The right-hand column of Table 7.2 shows the hypothetical returns from 1970 through 2004 of putting all four of these asset classes together and rebalancing them every year. As you can see, the balanced (and rebalanced) portfolio would have been less risky than a portfolio made up of any one of the four components. And its cumulative return beat three of those four components.

Figure 7.8 (The Balance of S&P 500 Index versus U.S. Small-

Cap Stocks) is modeled on some of the graphs we introduced in Chapter 6. As you can see, for the period in the study, U.S. small-cap stocks were significantly more productive and also significantly more risky than large-cap stocks. But the curved line on the chart also shows that a 50/50 combination provided more return, at less risk, than the average of the two, which would fall on the midpoint of a straight line connecting the two ends of the curve. It's another example of what I call smart diversification.

We're now ready to take the next step in building Your Perfect Portfolio by splitting the equity slice of the pie into equal parts of large-cap U.S. stocks (represented by the S&P 500 Index) and small-cap U.S. stocks. To represent small-cap stocks we use the results of the Dimensional Fund Advisors U.S. Micro Cap Fund, which invests in the 9th and 10th deciles of the U.S. stock market.

The result is presented in Figure 7.9, called Portfolio 3. This step adds 1.4 percentage points to the return of Portfolio 2. But at

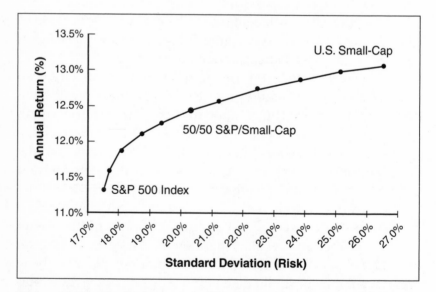

Figure 7.8   The Balance of S&P 500 versus U.S. Small-Cap Stocks (1970–2004)

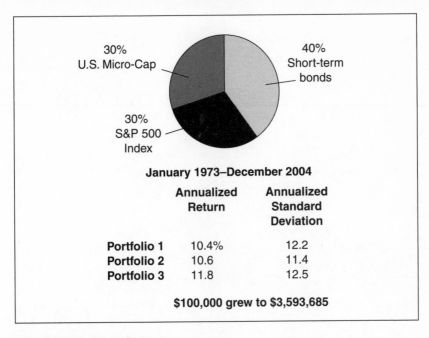

Figure 7.9   Portfolio 3

the same time, its standard deviation has increased, indicating higher volatility than the benchmark portfolio.

This means we have more work ahead to achieve our goal of a higher return at lower risk. We'll get to that work in the next two chapters.

At this point, it's worth noting that the two simple changes we have made so far have added $1,195,814 to the long-term results of the standard pension fund, with only a slight amount of additional risk.

Chapter EIGHT

Value: Owning What Others Don't Want

■■■■■■

The word crisis in Chinese is composed of two characters. The first is the symbol of danger, the second the symbol of opportunity.

—Unknown

One of the most fundamental mistakes investors make is paying high prices for popular assets. The message of this chapter is that you should invest in stocks that other investors don't want, stocks whose prices may have been going down instead of up.

It's a pity more investors don't behave like good shoppers. If they did, they'd look for opportunities to snap up good assets when they're on sale. The good news is that an important part of what investors need is always on sale.

According to the strange logic followed by so many investors, it's apparently better to pay full price for stocks, or even pay more than full price, when everybody else wants them, instead of buying them when they're on sale. This is one of the main reasons so many investors found themselves in deep trouble in 2000, 2001, and 2002. Back in the late 1990s, they bought technology and telecommunications stocks as if the price they paid didn't matter.

To oversimplify somewhat, you can say the universe of stocks is divided into two parts: growth stocks and value stocks. When they are owned properly, value stocks pay more than growth stocks. Growth stocks represent excellent companies that inspire pride and hope. These companies tend to have good management, good products, strong financial positions, rising sales, rising profits, and rising prospects. Not coincidentally, they often have rising stock prices, too. Value stocks represent companies that are "unexcellent" and unpopular for any number of reasons. They may be in dead-end industries. They may have made big mistakes. They may be saddled with terrific competition, crummy management, and obsolete products.

So what's not to like about growth companies? The companies themselves are often wonderful. So wonderful that investors have bid their stock prices up to levels at which Wall Street must expect—and even demand—that these companies keep churning out nearly miraculous results. One slip, and billions of dollars of stock market value can be wiped out in a few minutes.

And what's good about value stocks? The one thing you can say about them for sure is that they are cheap. They let investors buy low, the critical (and often overlooked) part of the time-tested formula: Buy low, sell high.

Am I saying you should buy some "dog" stocks and pay for them by selling perennial favorites like Microsoft and Merck? Not at all. Smart investors don't buy value stocks one by one. There are almost always valid reasons why any particular value stock is out of favor. The best way to buy value stocks is by the hundreds, through mutual funds that specialize in them. Buy the whole asset class, and you won't lose sleep when a handful of these companies bite the dust.

The folks on Wall Street are by no means stupid, and a portfolio full of value stocks will inevitably contain plenty of dogs. If you make a list of today's top value stocks, after five years you'll probably find at least half of the same stocks on the list (and some will be out of business). If you buy only a handful of value stocks, you could easily wind up entirely invested in companies that deserve permanent "value" status, and in that case you won't get the premium return you expect for investing in value companies. But if you buy the whole asset class and hold it long enough, you'll likely be glad you did. Over the years, a large group of value stocks will almost certainly outperform an equally large group of popular growth stocks.

Why is this true? It comes back to the basic formula of how investing works. Investors get paid for taking risks. Value stocks are more risky than more popular growth stocks. Fortunately, mutual funds that invest in these stocks give investors a way to cash in on the gains while mitigating most of the risks.

Virtually all the famous investment managers of the past 50 years (Warren Buffett, Peter Lynch, Ben Graham, Bill Miller) made their marks by investing in value stocks. Shouldn't you pay attention to their examples?

If you don't believe in the concept of buying low and selling high, it's pretty hard to know what you should do instead. But if you do believe in buying low and selling high, then you'll have to be willing to take opportunities to buy assets when their prices are low. When prices are declining and nobody seems to want that asset, it takes a strong leap of faith to buy it. This faith, when it's based on knowledge of the past, is one thing that separates successful investors from frustrated ones.

Identifying small-cap stocks is pretty easy. But identifying value stocks is trickier, because there are many ways to measure value. The basic point is that value stocks are bargains. Bargain investments are often measured subjectively by estimating their future values based on expectations for future performance. Many value investors believe a stock is a good buy if it's likely it will return to its "normal" level when investors come to their senses. I don't like to rely on human judgment that much, and fortunately that isn't necessary. Investors can get the benefits of value investing by adopting a mechanical method for identifying value stocks.

This mechanical approach starts by identifying the largest 50 percent of stocks traded on the New York Stock Exchange and all other public companies of similar size, based on their market capitalization. The companies are then sorted by the ratio of their price per share to their book value per share. (Book value represents the total value of a company's assets on its balance sheet. In a rough way, it values the business not as a going concern but as a collection of assets that could be sold at an industrial garage sale.)

The top 30 percent of stocks on this list, those with the highest price-to-book ratios, are classified as growth companies. The theory is that they are valued by investors more for their future profitability than for the assets they own. The bottom 30 percent of stocks on the list are classified as large-cap value companies. A similar process can be used to identify small-cap value stocks.

Although growth stocks are the most popular ones (and almost universally regarded as the "safest" investments), much research shows that historically, unpopular (value) stocks outperform popular (growth) ones.

The best academic research I'm aware of— studies by Dr. Eugene Fama of the University of Chicago and Dr. Kenneth French of Yale—provides the numbers.

Among U.S. large company stocks, from 1927 through 2004, growth stocks had an annualized total return of 9.4 percent; value stocks grew at a rate of 11.8 percent. What does that mean in real terms? Over a 40-year period, it's the difference between turning an initial investment of $10,000 into $363,658 (growth stocks) or $866,308 (value stocks).

Among U.S. small-company issues from 1927 through 2004, growth stocks grew at 9.4 percent, value stocks at 14.8 percent. That's the difference over a 40-year period between turning $10,000 into $363,658 (growth stocks) or into $2,498,478 (value stocks). The academics say this same relationship has been found time after time in stocks traded in virtually every country in the world. The one exception is in Italy; the researchers haven't figured out why that country is an anomaly.

Value stocks have another terrific attribute: They behave differently from growth stocks. You can see this clearly in Figure 8.1, which compares returns from the S&P 500 Index with those of large-cap value stocks from 1974 through 2004. The 50/50 combination we recommend, as you can see, adds about 1.6 percentage points of return to the S&P 500 Index while reducing risk nicely from the large value index.

Of course, not all value companies will turn out to be worth owning. When you go shopping, you know that not everything

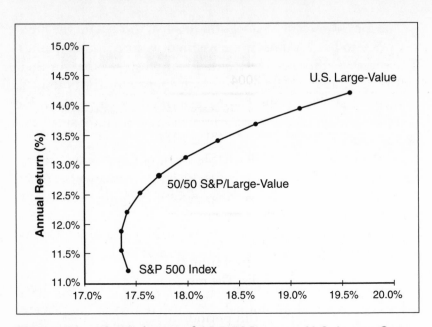

Figure 8.1   The Balance of S&P 500 versus U.S. Large-Cap Stocks (1970–2004)

with a low price is a true bargain. Many stock analysts spend virtually all their time trying to figure out which stocks are underpriced and which aren't—and most of them fail to continually and repeatedly beat the indexes. Even full-time professionals make plenty of mistakes, and you're likely to do the same if you try this on your own. Unless you're a professional, the best way to buy value stocks is to buy lots of them, through index funds.

How Reliable Are Value Stocks?

In each of the previous two chapters, we cited a study of many years of market history and presented partial results in tables like Table 8.1. This table focuses on the premium

---

Table 8.1

Value Premiums, 1926–2004

Period	1 year	5 years	10 years	15 years	20 years	25 years
Best	129	299	681	1,909	3,119	8,116
Average	4.8	38.4	152	454	1,149	2,702
Worst	−66.2	−178	−228	−217	−13.9	158
Reliability	63.2%	78.9%	87.1%	92.4%	99.1%	100%

return investors may expect from value stocks when compared with growth stocks. The meaning of these data is explained in Chapter 6.

Table 8.1 shows that in periods of a single year, value stocks had an average advantage of 4.8 percentage points over growth stocks. And while some premium occurred in more than six out of every ten possible one-year periods, value stocks were sometimes far, far behind—as you can see from the worst 12-month period, in which value stocks returned 66 percentage points less than growth stocks.

We saw in earlier chapters that longer periods produced larger and more reliable premium returns from investing in equities instead of T-bills and from investing in small-cap stocks instead of large-cap ones. Table 8.1 shows that the same holds true with value stocks. As you can see in the "15 years" column, as long as you held value stocks for at least 15 years, in nine times out of 10 you would achieve a higher return. And the premium was virtually guaranteed with a 20-year holding period.

This is why it makes good sense to include growth stocks in your portfolio as well as value stocks.

Incidentally, value investing works with international stocks, too, although the data do not go back quite as far as for U.S. stocks. From 1975 through 2004, an index of international value stocks appreciated at an annual rate of 17.7 percent. By contrast, an index of large company international stocks (mostly growth companies) rose at a rate of 12.1 percent.

In short, if you're looking for long-term results above those that come from following the crowd, you're likely to find them from owning value stocks.

The next step in building Your Perfect Portfolio is shown in Figure 8.2, called Portfolio 4. To take this step, we split the equity side of the pie into four slices instead of two, adding U.S. large value stocks and U.S. small value stocks. This boosts the annualized return of the portfolio to 12.6 percent, while reducing the standard deviation to 12.3 percent.

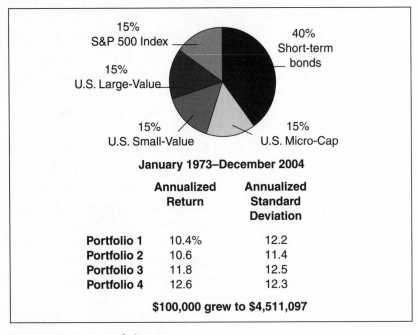

January 1973–December 2004

	Annualized Return	Annualized Standard Deviation
Portfolio 1	10.4%	12.2
Portfolio 2	10.6	11.4
Portfolio 3	11.8	12.5
Portfolio 4	12.6	12.3

$100,000 grew to $4,511,097

Figure 8.2   Portfolio 4

This is an extremely significant improvement, because we have boosted return by 21 percent with virtually no change in volatility.

Some investors might be quite content to stop here, having raised the annual return by 21 percent and the 32-year returns by 88 percent to $4,511,097, at about the same volatility. But there's one more very important step in creating Your Perfect Portfolio. We'll discuss it in the next chapter.

Chapter NINE

Putting the World to Work for You

■■■■■

The world is a book, and he who stays at home reads only one page.

—M.K. Frelinghuysen

A recurring piece of nonsense that's taught to many investors is that they can get all the investment performance they'll ever need or want from companies based in the United States. Only about half of the world's stock market value resides in companies based in the United States. The rest is beyond the U.S. borders. Throughout this book, I urge investors to diversify. That's the most fundamental piece of investment advice I know. I believe almost all investors should have some exposure to international stocks.

The stocks of companies with headquarters outside the

United States don't always outperform those of U.S. companies. But there are years—and multiyear periods—in which U.S. stocks take a back seat to international ones. That's why I counsel investors, including my company's clients, to have half their equity investments in international funds.

One of the biggest risks investors take is believing too strongly that they know what they are doing—overconfidence, if you will. Investors in Japan in 1990 had every legitimate reason to believe that they didn't need to invest in stocks outside their own country, which at the time was on the brink of having the world's largest economy.

Nobody could have credibly predicted that the bottom would fall out of the Japanese market for the next dozen or more years. Yet that's exactly what happened. Japanese investors whose capital was tied up exclusively in their own country's stocks paid a terrible price. Coming from the lips of an adviser or an investor, "It can't happen here" is an invitation for trouble.

Even if international stocks do not outperform their U.S. counterparts, they provide a frequently overlooked but intensely valuable diversification benefit to retirees who are regularly taking money from their portfolios. In fact, as we show, international stocks can make the difference between a retirement portfolio that lasts a lifetime and one that runs out of money prematurely.

As we show in this chapter, adding international stocks to Your Perfect Portfolio finishes the job of creating an investment combination with higher returns and lower risks than the standard pension fund model.

I've been asked why I recommend splitting the equity part of a portfolio equally between U.S. and international stocks. The answer is simplicity itself: because it works, for many legitimate reasons.

Many people are wary of investing outside the United States, partly from fear of the unknown. Some investment gurus have found a ready audience for the idea that investors can fully participate in the global economy if they own shares of large U.S.-based multinational companies that do a great deal of their business overseas. Prominent examples are Coca-Cola, Microsoft, and McDonald's.

It's true that international business is quite important to these companies. But anybody who owns an S&P 500 Index fund has plenty of exposure to companies like that. Owning more of them, in the name of international investing, is really little more than piling on more large-cap U.S. growth stocks.

We will see in this chapter that over long periods of time (and in many short periods as well), international stocks have outperformed U.S. stocks. But you shouldn't include them in your portfolio primarily for a premium return. You should include them in your portfolio because they reduce risk when they're combined with U.S. stocks.

Now of course I know that investing internationally makes a lot of people skittish. And I know you will make up your own mind what to do. But before you dismiss the idea out of hand, I hope you'll join me while we examine the most obvious risk of owning an equity portfolio based exclusively in the United States.

Let's look at a bit of fairly recent history. In the late 1980s and 1990s, it was obvious to anybody who read the newspapers that Japan was on a meteoric economic rise. Japan's economy, the second largest in the world, seemed to be on the brink of threatening the United States for the number 1 position. Japanese tourists seemed to have buckets of money to spend in North America. Japanese money propped up the sale of U.S. Treasury securities.

Many people were startled when Japanese interests purchased an American icon in New York City, Rockefeller Center. Some developers predicted that U.S. business parks specializing in technology companies would soon be accessible by freeway exit ramps with Japanese names like "Fuji Blvd." Some of this may seem silly today, but it was credible at the time.

Now imagine you were an investor working and living in Japan in 1990. If you were prudent, you might have thought about buying stocks in large U.S. companies. But you probably would have been scoffed at. You might have been told something like this: "There's no need to invest outside Japan; everything you need is right here, and we are leading the world."

That must have sounded very credible. But an unfortunate thing happened on the way to this promised nirvana: It didn't pan out. The Japanese Nikkei index started falling, on its way from 38,916 yen in December 1989 to a low of 7,752 yen in April 2003. Japan had a thriving mutual fund industry, but 90 percent of that industry's assets disappeared in losses and redemptions. While Japanese stocks went into this major spiral throughout the 1990s, the U.S. stock market had one of its best decades ever.

The numbers: From 1990 through 2004, large-company stocks in Japan (including such "safe" companies as Sony, Toyota, and Mitsubishi) had a negative annual compound return of 3.4 percent. That's a figure that has a minus sign in front of it, and it's compounded over 15 years. That rate of return reduced a 1,000-yen investment to 595 yen. Think of the shattered dreams that loss represents. Remember, that resulted from investing in an asset class—large Japanese companies—that was widely regarded as "a sure thing." Small-company Japanese stocks in the same 15 years had a negative annualized return of 2.9 percent, a rate that would have reduced 1,000 yen to 674 yen. Imagine how this would have felt to a retiree depending on Japanese equity funds.

When we consulted the Morningstar database in 2004, we found seven Japanese stock funds that had track records of 10 years or longer. Their average 10-year annualized return was a negative 1.26 percent. So I am now giving the same counsel to you, presumably a U.S.-based investor, that millions of Japanese investors must wish they had heeded in 1990: No matter how high your confidence level is, don't invest all your money in your own country.

The key question is how much international exposure an investor should have. After extensive study of this issue, we believe that 50/50 is an excellent choice for most investors. By splitting your equities equally between U.S. and international funds, you essentially say, "Why choose?"

Investing in Global and Worldwide Funds

Many mutual fund companies manage funds that include both U.S. and international stocks, hoping to attract investors who want a one-fund package to give them all they need.

Unfortunately, such funds aren't a good substitute for international funds. Typically, global and worldwide funds have a significant minority—and sometimes it's the majority—of their portfolios in U.S.-based stocks.

The giant American Funds New Perspective Fund (ANWPX) has 38 percent of its assets in U.S. stocks. The $1.1 billion Fidelity Worldwide Fund (FWWFX) has 53 percent of its portfolio in U.S. stocks. For the Dreyfus Premier Worldwide Growth Fund (DPWRX), the percentage in U.S. stocks is 60 percent.

We looked at 10 of the largest funds in Morningstar's "world stock" category and found that on average, they kept 39.6 percent of their assets in U.S. equities. This means they won't give investors the international diversification they need. In addition, such funds are almost always filled primarily with large growth-oriented companies. That further detracts from proper diversification.

In our view, the best advice regarding worldwide and global stock funds is to "just say no."

How did we come to that conclusion? It was simple: We used the lessons of the past as our best guide. We have reliable data that go back to the 1950s for international stocks, giving us a window into history that's large enough to see long-term patterns.

Almost all investors go through two distinct phases: accumulation and withdrawal. International stocks contribute to the results in each one, but in different ways, so we'll examine them separately.

On the web site for this book, www.wiley.com/go/paul merriman, there's a table (available there as Table 9.1A) that shows year-by-year returns starting in January 1970 (and updated through the latest whole calendar year) for two all-equity portfolios. The first portfolio had no international funds; the second was made up of half U.S. funds and half international funds.

Let's see what the numbers say. In Table 9.1, we show the bottom-line results of these two portfolios for 35 years, from 1970 through 2004. As you can see, an initial investment of $10,000 in the all-U.S. portfolio grew to $676,837 by the end of 2004, while the same investment in the 50/50 portfolio grew to $980,308. What you can't see here (but you'll find in the table on the web site) is that the su-

Table 9.1

Equity Investing With and Without International Stocks, 1970–2004

	All U.S. equities	50% international equities 50% U.S. equities
Annualized return	12.8%	14.0%
$10,000 grew to	$676,837	$980,308
Standard deviation	20.0%	16.8%
Worst month	−25.2%	−18.8%
Worst 12 months	−34.3%	−35.1%
Worst 36 months	−37.1%	−23.8%
Worst 60 months	−28.5%	−10.9%

periority of the more diversified portfolio established itself quickly and never faded.

After just two years, at the end of 1971, the 50/50 combination was worth $12,615, versus only $11,368 for the all-U.S. portfolio. After 10 years, the lead was greater: $34,315 versus $24,155. And after 20 years, at the end of 1989, there was no race any more. The 50/50 portfolio was worth $210,088, far ahead of the U.S. portfolio, $114,520.

This is not a fluke that's limited to results starting in 1970. We calculated a total of twenty-one 15-year returns for these portfolios (one starting in 1970, another in 1971, another in 1972, etc.) and found that the 50/50 combination outperformed the all-U.S. portfolio in 17 of those 21 periods.

As you can see in Table 9.1, return is only part of the story. The table shows that the 50/50 combination had less risk by every measurement except the worst 12 months.

In my workshops, I show a table with more columns, one for each 10 percent increment of international stocks: 10 percent, 20 percent, 30 percent, and so on. In every case, the larger the percentage of international funds, the greater the return. (This table is available on this book's web site as Figure 9.2A. It's called "How Much Should You Invest in International Equities?")

I believe a 50/50 mix of U.S. and international equity funds is suitable for most people. Moving from a mix of all U.S. equities to an all-international portfolio over the 35 years covered in Table 9.1 added 1.7 percentage points of return. A 50/50 mix captured 1.2 of those percentage points, while reducing risk to its lowest point among all 11 combinations.

In those 35 years, an initial investment of $100,000 in Portfolio 4 (see Figure 8.2 in the previous chapter) would have grown to $5.1 million. That's without any international exposure. But when half the equity part of the portfolio was in international funds, the same initial investment grew to $7.3 million. This was a 43 percent increase in the ultimate return, and it came from changing only 30 percent of the portfolio. Think about that the next time you read or hear that international funds aren't worth your time.

I could fill half of this book with other examples to show that international equity investing works. Here's something I wrote in a newsletter to investors at the start of 2004:

"Last year the Standard & Poor's 500 Index was up 28.5 percent, its best year since 1998. Our recommended equity portfolio of eight Vanguard index funds was up 42 percent. One important reason that recommended portfolio did so well was that half of it was invested in international funds. Many investment advisers apparently don't think investors deserve results that good. They recommend only 10 to 15 percent of an equity portfolio be in international funds."

In 2003, the U.S. component of our equity portfolio gained 35.9 percent. The international part was up 48.3 percent. This wasn't something new. The international component of this portfolio had outshined the U.S. part in three of the previous five calendar years, from 1999 through 2003. In 1999, the U.S. index funds in this group were up 15.1 percent while the international ones gained 50.2 percent. In the awful year of 2002, when the U.S. index funds lost 19.3 percent, the international ones lost only 12.9 percent.

If you still aren't sure of the value of international funds, please join me in looking at the difference that they make to the typical retiree. We'll take up the topic of portfolio withdrawals in much more detail in Chapter 12. But this chapter would not be complete without making the point that international funds can play a special role for retirees. The key concept for the moment is volatility.

When investors are accumulating assets, volatility may be uncomfortable, but it doesn't actually hurt unless it spooks those investors into abandoning a good strategy. But for investors who are regularly withdrawing money from their portfolios, volatility is a major threat.

Let me state four basic points before I back them up with a table of figures.

1. The biggest risk that retirees face is running out of money prematurely—in other words, before they run out of life.

2. A portfolio that's being asked to support regular with-drawals—especially withdrawals that increase over the years to keep up with inflation—has very different needs than a portfolio that's merely trying to accumulate assets.

3. Stability—the lack of big losses—is critical in keeping such a portfolio alive for many years. Even one terrible year can ruin things.

4. International stocks provide the stability that can make that difference.

Table 9.2 shows the year-by-year results for three variations of a balanced portfolio, half of which remains in short-term bond funds. I believe this is a suitable allocation for retired people who want a reasonable combination of high returns (from equities) and low volatility (from fixed-income funds).

The table shows three variations, with international stocks making up zero, 15 percent, and 25 percent of the whole portfolio. (That's equivalent to zero, 30 percent, and half of the equity part of the portfolio.) The figures in each column represent the value of the portfolio at the end of the year.

This table is oriented toward taking fixed annual withdrawals in retirement. We generated this table assuming you started with $1 million at the start of 1970 and took out $60,000 for living expenses at the start of the year. We further assumed that at the start of each subsequent year, you withdrew 3.5 percent more than you had in the previous year, thus $62,100 for living expenses in 1971, $64,274 for 1972, and so forth. This corresponds to an assumed inflation rate of 3.5 percent per year.

The purpose of Table 9.2 is to show the value that international funds can make in a retirement portfolio.

The good news is that none of these three variations came even close to running out of money. The disturbing news is that in the early 1970s, the portfolio with no international equity funds lost 26 percent of its initial value (as it fell to $735,685).

In my experience, most retirees would not be likely to stay the course after losing 26 percent of their money. And unfortunately,

Table 9.2

Retiring on $1 Million with and without International Equities

Withdrawal at start of each year		0% international	15% international	25% international
$ 60,000	1970	$ 995,461	$ 988,585	$ 983,482
$ 62,100	1971	$1,043,156	$1,072,879	$1,092,014
$ 64,274	1972	$1,038,111	$1,120,799	$1,177,942
$ 66,523	1973	$ 872,810	$ 965,556	$1,030,350
$ 68,851	1974	$ 735,685	$ 816,759	$ 872,609
$ 71,261	1975	$ 859,937	$ 956,726	$1,022,048
$ 73,755	1976	$ 999,494	$1,072,939	$1,117,778
$ 76,337	1977	$ 961,458	$1,091,953	$1,179,789
$ 79,009	1978	$ 963,911	$1,157,687	$1,294,997
$ 81,774	1979	$1,051,696	$1,238,452	$1,363,749
$ 84,636	1980	$1,143,706	$1,367,230	$1,517,034
$ 87,598	1981	$1,201,177	$1,441,264	$1,598,697
$ 90,664	1982	$1,392,883	$1,639,688	$1,790,424
$ 93,837	1983	$1,569,361	$1,855,073	$2,026,347
$ 97,122	1984	$1,568,161	$1,890,347	$2,087,014
$100,521	1985	$1,804,911	$2,279,748	$2,588,614
$104,039	1986	$1,924,884	$2,602,796	$3,082,079
$107,681	1987	$1,866,425	$2,698,906	$3,328,269
$111,449	1988	$2,001,759	$2,982,734	$3,732,599
$115,350	1989	$2,149,161	$3,312,763	$4,216,069
$119,387	1990	$1,919,315	$3,072,790	$3,983,826
$123,566	1991	$2,227,404	$3,588,814	$4,634,938
$127,891	1992	$2,365,877	$3,734,764	$4,721,773
$132,367	1993	$2,519,439	$4,183,494	$5,430,691
$137,000	1994	$2,353,327	$4,036,309	$5,312,796
$141,795	1995	$2,707,197	$4,604,042	$5,969,078
$146,758	1996	$2,929,532	$5,004,276	$6,452,126
$151,894	1997	$3,255,777	$5,372,257	$6,710,529
$157,210	1998	$3,310,779	$5,591,807	$7,039,942
$162,713	1999	$3,470,703	$6,090,372	$7,801,219
$168,408	2000	$3,456,124	$6,070,777	$7,713,467
$174,302	2001	$3,526,904	$6,149,490	$7,703,284
$180,402	2002	$3,214,747	$5,829,475	$7,424,935
$186,717	2003	$3,690,665	$6,946,981	$8,966,942
$193,252	2004	$3,826,850	$7,491,266	$9,816,841
Total withdrawals		**$4,000,441**	**$4,000,441**	**$4,000,441**

when people bail out, they often become easy prey for financial salespeople—sometimes with disastrous results.

The portfolio with 25 percent in international stocks, by contrast, had lost only about 13 percent of its initial value by the end of 1974. That is *half* the loss of the all-U.S. variation and much more likely to be tolerable.

Staying the course was the only way to reap the considerable rewards that lay ahead for these hypothetical investors. The portfolio with 25 percent in international stocks gave retirees a higher probability of staying the course, along with a much richer reward for doing so: $9.8 million versus $3.8 million for the all-U.S. version.

Let's move to Figure 9.1 (The Balance of U.S. versus International Funds, 1974–2004). You'll see right away that the S&P 500 Index had a higher return than the Morgan Stanley Europe Australia Far East Index (EAFE). But you'll see that a 50/50 combination of the two gave you most of that extra return while

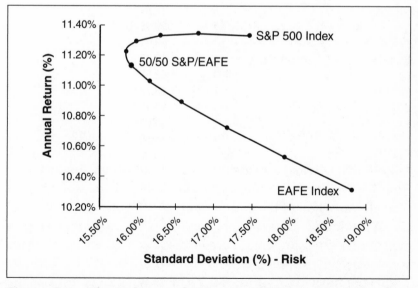

Figure 9.1 The Balance of U.S. versus International Funds, 1970–2004

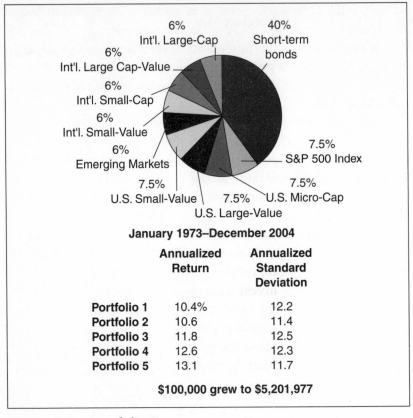

Figure 9.2   Portfolio 5

substantially reducing the volatility of each of those components.

With that, we're ready to take the final step in putting together
Your Perfect Portfolio. You see this in Figure 9.2, Portfolio 5. This
step allocates half of the equities part of the portfolio to international funds and splits that portion five ways, including a 6 percent slice of emerging markets (see box). As you can see, in these
four relatively simple steps, we have added 2.7 percentage
points of return to this portfolio, an increase of 26 percent, while

Emerging Markets Funds

The best way to diversify an equity portfolio is to include assets that have a good chance of providing premium returns at reasonable risk. Ideally, they should not be highly correlated with the overall market. At least in theory, emerging markets funds meet both those tests.

Emerging markets represent the great growth potential of young economies. Think of the difference between IBM and Microsoft in the late 1980s.

The majority of the world's people live and work in emerging-markets countries, places like Brazil, Chile, Poland, Hungary, and Russia. The average age of their populations is lower than those of most developed countries. As these younger populations mature, millions of their people will turn into new investors and begin thinking about their retirement. That will raise the demand for stocks, which should in turn raise stock prices. There's potential for a number of other areas of the world to experience the type of stock market boom that flourished in the United States during the 1990s.

Emerging markets funds can be quite profitable. From 1988 through 2004, an emerging markets index compiled by Dimensional Fund Advisors appreciated at an annual rate of 15.6 percent, compared with 12 percent for the S&P 500 Index. A Vanguard emerging markets index fund rose 61 percent in 1999 and 57 percent in 2003.

On the other hand, emerging markets can take investors on a wild ride that's not suited for timid souls. Vanguard's fund fell by 16.8 percent in 1997 and dropped another 18.1 percent in 1998; it fell by 27 percent in 2000. In addition, less stringent accounting standards, scarce information, and lax laws all combine to make emerging markets stocks riskier investments than those of developed countries.

There are two ways investors can tame the high volatility of emerging markets. First, by using no-load mutual funds that diversify widely instead of concentrating on a single region such as Russia or Latin America. And second, by limiting these funds to no more than 10 percent of the equity part of a portfolio.

Emerging markets may be the frosting. But they are not the cake.

we reduced the risk. The theoretical payoff for a $100,000 investment rose from $2.4 million to nearly $5.2 million.

At this point, you know how to build a portfolio that will harness a world of investment opportunities to help you reach your goals.

Chapter TEN

Controlling Risks

■■■■■

Trust in Allah, but tie your camel.

—*Arab proverb*

A recurring theme throughout this book is risk, and finally the topic gets its own chapter. I haven't consolidated every part of the risk discussion into one place because it is a topic that needs to be brought up again and again. I hope you'll get used to thinking of it as an integral part of investing. In this chapter we move from risk as an abstract concept to risk as a cold, hard reality with specific numbers. There's no perfect way to know in advance precisely what level of loss you can tolerate, but there are numerous ways to help you get a handle on it.

One of the most important things we do in my company is interview prospective and new clients about their risk tolerance. In a confidential client information form, we ask a series of questions that help us to get an authentic look at how each person deals with adversity. In some cases we ask the same question more than once, just in different ways.

Ultimately, it's necessary to get specific about making the trade-offs between risk and expected return. In workshops and with clients, we use a table of numbers to show the results (in the past, because that's all we had) of various combinations of equity funds and fixed-income funds, each with its own set of returns and risks.

With this table, an investor who has carefully thought about his or her needs and risk tolerance can choose a combination of investments that's likely to provide the right combination of growth and comfort.

In many years of counseling individual investors, I've seen again and again how tough it is for people to know in advance how much risk they can actually stomach. Your risk tolerance has a large emotional (and therefore somewhat unpredictable) component.

In the abstract, risk is elusive. When you're basking in the warmth of summer, it's hard to be too serious about the warm clothes you'll need in winter. And when you're dreaming of a pleasant and prosperous retirement, it's easy to gloss over the fact that you could fairly easily lose half your money if you make the wrong investments.

In practice, your risk tolerance is probably more complex than a single number. Most people have to make monthly mortgage payments. I don't think they have much tolerance for risking the money earmarked for that next mortgage payment. On the other hand, if you're saving for a goal 10 to 20 years in the future, the prospect of an interim loss should be less worrisome.

In my own case, I have three portfolios, each with its own risk tolerance. I have a very conservatively invested portfolio of money set aside for my retirement. Although I hope I won't have to retire for many years, when the time comes I want to be sure that money is there to take care of me and my family. My risk tolerance for this money is very low.

My second portfolio is money I don't expect to ever need. I intend that it will someday go to my children, and it's invested aggressively to seek a high return, based on what I consider their risk tolerance, not mine.

My third portfolio is probably off the charts in terms of risk. Some people would consider this to be "play money." While I never buy individual stocks, from time to time I invest "for fun" in the ventures of friends and people I know. I don't expect a high return from these investments. Twice I have helped friends get started in the financial services business. And once I invested in a movie in which my son was involved.

I'm not suggesting you adopt my plan. But I do hope you'll realize that you may have more than a single pot of money with only one level of tolerance for risk. For example, I think some retirees short-change their children by being much too conservative with money that they (the parents) will never need.

In my workshop I ask how many participants are willing to lose half or more of their money. I see hands from only about one out of every 100 people. Then I ask how many people own individual stocks. Lots of hands go up. Warren Buffett and Peter Lynch, two legendary investors of the past 50 years, have both said that all-equity investors are likely to lose 50 percent of their money from time to time. The only conclusion I can draw is that many of the people who come to my workshops simply don't understand the level of risk they have been taking.

My company has developed an excellent tool that can help you figure out your own tolerance for risk. This is a very important part of the work we do with clients. We ask potential clients to complete a confidential questionnaire before our first interview so they can think about the issues. There are no right or wrong answers. The best answers are the most honest answers.

Here are 11 of the questions on this form, all related to risk, along with my thoughts on what the answers might indicate:

1. For a potential annual return of 8 to 10 percent, you would tolerate a maximum one-year loss of _____ percent.

2. For a potential annual return of 10 to 12 percent, you would tolerate a maximum one-year loss of _____ percent.

3. For a potential annual return of 12 to 15 percent, you would tolerate a maximum one-year loss of _____ percent.

   Comment: In my experience, most retirees can meet their needs with returns of 8 to 10 percent at very reasonable levels of risk. It's rare that any investor truly needs more than 10 to 12 percent, and we usually don't even need to ask the third question. But we do so in order to see if people understand that higher returns go hand in hand with higher levels of risk.

   Anybody who wants a return of 10 to 12 percent and can't tolerate an interim loss of more than 10 percent is heading for big trouble. If you need a 10 percent return, you should be prepared for a one-year loss of at least 15 percent. In seeking a return of 12 to 15 percent, you'd better be ready to lose 20 to 50 percent at some point along the way.

4. What past investments have you made that pleased you? Why did they please you?

   Comment: The answer to this question is always something that made money. And that is invariably something that's part of an asset class that was profitable at that time. Rarely do people say they were pleased with an investment because it had low risk.

5. What past investments did not please you? Why were you

displeased? Would you make a similar investment again? How did you respond to your displeasure with this investment?

Comment: The investments listed in answer to this question are invariably ones that either lost money or made much less than they "should have" in the view of the investor. The "why" question is a way to get investors to think about their own relationship with taking risks.

The third part of this question is particularly interesting. If you are willing to do something worthwhile (and for investors, taking risks is not only worthwhile but necessary) a second time, even after being burned the first time, you may truly understand the concept of risk.

Sometimes the same investment, for example an S&P 500 Index fund, is listed as the answer to both question 3 and question 4, the only difference being the timing of the investment. (The Vanguard 500 Index Fund severely disappointed many investors with a 22.2 percent loss in 2002; but it must have thoroughly delighted many investors with its 28.5 percent gain in 2003.)

The final part of this question is the all-important one. The most accurate indicator of your actual risk tolerance is probably what you will do in the face of adversity. And your past actions are a strong indicator of your likely future actions.

If you made and followed a thoughtful plan for dealing with losses, that suggests you have a healthy understanding of risk and can deal with it well. But if you looked at the newspapers one day and sold in panic after suddenly realizing you had lost money, that suggests you should not be exposed to high levels of risk.

6. On a scale of 1 to 10, with 1 being extremely conservative and 10 extremely aggressive, how would you characterize yourself as an investor?

Comment: People who rate themselves 7 and above usually believe they are able to accept quite a bit of risk. However, we often find that the answer to this question is inconsistent with other answers. This indicates that more discussion is warranted.

This question is a good example of something else that's useful about this quiz. Many times we'll find that the questions are answered differently by a husband and wife. When the differences are significant, this gives us a chance to start a conversation that can help a couple see that their risk tolerance may not be as straightforward as they (or as one of them) previously thought.

7. Choose the statement that best describes your overall investment objectives:

▪ Growing assets without concern for current income

▪ Growing assets somewhat, while generating current income

▪ Generating current income and preserving capital

Comment: This question is carefully worded to force an investor to make a choice rather than indicate a desire for every possible result. It's also helpful to see whether or not the answer to this question is consistent with other answers.

8. If you invested $100,000 seeking a long-term return of 10 to 12 percent, choose the maximum short-term (one-year) loss you would accept:

▪ More than $15,000

▪ $10,000 to $15,000

▪ Less than $10,000

Comment: This is essentially the same as the first question on our list. We include it in order to see if the answer matches the earlier answer. What we're looking for is consistency (or the lack of it). Sometimes people believe they are willing to tolerate percentage losses that they won't accept when those losses are stated in real dollars.

We once had a client who was certain he could tolerate a loss of 10 percent of his portfolio. But panic unexpectedly struck him after a loss of only 4 percent. The reason: That 4 percent was equal to the number of dollars he was accustomed to earning in a full year. That thought was simply too tough for him emotionally.

9. Indicate when you expect to need (or plan to use) the money you are investing or have invested:

   ▨ 10 or more years

   ▨ 6 to 10 years

   ▨ Less than 6 years

   Comment: This gives us some essential information. Money that will be needed in only a few years should not be exposed to large potential losses. On the other hand, an investor who won't need money for decades should not be obsessively concerned with short-term comfort.

10. Pick one of the following statements

    ▨ I am willing to tolerate substantial swings in my portfolio value to maximize growth.

    ▨ I am willing to tolerate small swings in my portfolio value, though this might mean lower growth.

    ▨ I am willing to tolerate only slight deviations in my portfolio value despite slower overall growth.

    Comment: This is merely one more way to ask the question that we've been posing again and again. This is a "feeling" approach to the question instead of one based strictly on numbers. An investor who's at peace with the trade-off between risk and return will answer most of the questions on this form in a consistent manner. More often, we see somewhat different answers when we pose the question in different ways.

11. Pick one of the following:

    ▨ After investing, I generally know that ups and downs are inevitable and check the results infrequently.

■ After investing, I generally pay attention but recognize that values change constantly and do not worry excessively.

■ After investing, I generally watch the markets daily and calculate my gains or losses frequently.

Comment: The third choice is a red flag for us. An investor who tallies up gains and losses every day may be simply a meticulous bookkeeper. But he or she might be extremely nervous. Whatever it is, we want to understand the reason.

No single question on this list does the whole job. But when all these questions are honestly and thoughtfully answered and discussed, they provide an excellent window into an investor's ability to deal with risk. Unfortunately, most financial advisers don't take the time to go over these topics very thoroughly with their clients. I wish more of them did. If you have thoughtfully completed these steps, you're ready to get down to numbers.

We've already thoroughly covered equity diversification as a way to reduce risk. Beyond that, the most important thing you can do to control the level of risk you take is to adjust the mix of fixed-income and equity investments in your portfolio. This adjustment is one of the most fundamental decisions faced by every investor. Some investors prefer a total equity portfolio for its superior growth prospects. Others invest exclusively in fixed-income funds, wanting to completely avoid the risks of the stock market.

For most people, comfort and need intersect somewhere between those two extremes. How far should you go in one direction or the other? One excellent place to start your search is with a 50/50 mix of equity funds and bond funds. It's easy to understand and to keep balanced. And I have found that it works very well for people who are retired or nearing retirement.

A 50/50 split isn't for everybody, of course. Fortunately there is a wide range of possibilities. You'll see examples of this in Table 10.1, which contains some important numbers for in-

Table 10.1

Balancing Risk and Return, 1970–2004

Global equity percent	Fixed- income percent	Annualized return	Standard deviation	Worst 12 months	Worst 60 months
0	100	7.5%	3.4%	–2.8%	20.4%
10	90	8.3%	3.6%	–2.8%	23.1%
20	80	9.0%	4.4%	–3.0%	20.7%
30	70	9.7%	5.6%	–6.3%	16.8%
40	60	10.4%	7.0%	–10.9%	12.9%
50	50	11.0%	8.5%	–15.4%	9.0%
60	40	11.7%	10.1%	–19.7%	5.0%
70	30	12.3%	11.7%	–23.8%	1.0%
80	20	12.9%	13.4%	–27.7%	–2.9%
90	10	13.5%	15.1%	–31.5%	–6.9%
100	0	14.0%	16.8%	–35.1%	–10.9%

vestors. The numbers are excerpted from a more complete table that I use in my workshops and that is available on the web site for this book. (The full table includes year-by-year results of these combinations as well as two additional risk measurements for each: the worst 1-month and 36-month periods.)

Each line in the table represents a mix of global equities (along the lines described in Chapters 6 through 9) and fixed-income investments (as described at the end of Chapter 6). As you scroll down the page, each successive line includes an additional 10 percent incremental exposure to equities.

As you will see (and as you would probably expect), each additional dose of equities brings an increase in return and an increase in risk, represented here by standard deviation and worst 12-month and 60-month periods. The figures represent results from the years 1970 through 2004. (Worst periods are "rolling" measurements that don't necessarily correspond with calendar years. Each can start at the beginning of any calendar month. Thus April 1, 1998 through March 31, 1999 is one 12-month period.)

Notice that the 50/50 mix I recommend as a starting point achieved a compound annual return of 11 percent. That is 78 percent of the return of the 100 percent equity combination. The statistical risk of the 50/50 portfolio, a standard deviation of 8.5 percent, was about half that of the all-equity model. In other words, the 50/50 combination gave investors 78 percent of the gain with only half the pain. (Measured by the worst 12 months, the 50/50 portfolio reduced the pain by 55 percent.) The 60/40 mix (which we saw in Chapter 6 as the standard pension plan model) reduced the volatility of the all-equity portfolio by 40 percent while capturing 83 percent of the return.

In this 35-year period, an all-equity portfolio invested exclusively in the S&P 500 Index would have returned 11.3 percent. As this table shows, that was very close to the return of the 50/50 global equity combination.

Thus we see two ways investors could have earned essentially the same return. But of course those investors couldn't know that in advance, so risk becomes very important. Measured by its standard deviation of 17.4 percent, the S&P 500 Index was more than twice as risky as the globally diversified 50/50 combination.

The index subjected investors to a worst-12-month loss of 38.9 percent, versus only 16.1 percent for the 50/50 portfolio. The worst 60-month period ended with a cumulative loss of 17.5 percent for the index, compared with a gain of 9 percent for the 50/50 combination.

Getting the same return at greatly reduced risk might strike you as merely a nice idea. But I assure you, it's one of the most important concerns for retired people—and relatively few retirees understand it.

In my workshops, I present a large table based on a $1 million portfolio starting in 1970 with withdrawals of $60,000, increasing at the rate of 3.5 percent per year. (If this is starting to sound familiar, then you've been paying attention.) This table shows year-by-year results for 12 portfolios, ranging from all-fixed-income to 100 percent global equity, plus one that contains only the Standard & Poor's 500 Index.

I particularly like to compare the columns for the S&P 500 Index and the 50/50 combination, since they have produced nearly identical long-term returns. What's different about them is volatility, or risk. The S&P 500 Index is much more volatile, and in a retirement portfolio that is sometimes literally the kiss of death.

By January 2005, the Standard & Poor's 500 Index portfolio was totally broke. The 50/50 portfolio ended 2004 worth $9.8 million. That difference is the price of volatility.

The best way to use Table 10.1 is to start by writing down two numbers: the target return you need and your largest acceptable one-year loss in percentage terms. Start with the return figure and scan the table to find the line that would give you what you need. Check to see how the one-year loss stacks up against your wish. Assuming that is not a perfect match, find the line that matches your self-determined risk tolerance and you'll see the return you would have received. Can you find a way to achieve your goals with that return? If so, you've got a pretty good idea of the allocation that's likely to work for you.

But what if you need the returns from an allocation that has too much risk? Your first impulse may be to go for the desired return and figure you'll "tough it out" through the bad times. That's usually a big mistake. If your needs straddle two columns, you should choose the one that has the right level of risk.

There are three reasons for that. First, remember that the figures in this table are not predictions of the future, only results from the past. And the past is a more reliable indicator of risk than of returns. For any given combination of assets, the pattern of volatility will be more constant and more predictable than the pattern of return.

Second, risk matters much more than most people think, as the $11.7 million versus $358,000 example shows.

Finally, it is never acceptable or advisable to manage a portfolio in violation of your risk tolerance. Year after year, decade after decade, I have seen that the most common way that investors get in trouble is by taking more risk than they should. They're the ones who suffer serious losses and bail out when prices are down—just the opposite of what they should be doing if they were buying low and selling high.

If there's only one lesson you learn from this book, I hope it's this one: Never ignore your emotions or your "better judgment" in order to chase higher returns. If you prudently choose to take lower risks and wind up with a lower return, you might have to work longer before you can retire. You might have to spend less (and save more) before retiring. You might have to spend less after you retire.

In the end, peace of mind is priceless. You now have the tools at your disposal to get it from your investments.

Chapter ELEVEN

Meet Your Enemies: Expenses and Taxes

■■■■■

A small leak will sink a great ship.

—Benjamin Franklin

Investors should never forget that quotation from Ben Franklin. You can do everything else right, but if you let your investment gains leak out of your portfolio, your money won't be there when you need it.

Expenses and taxes are like leaks. Even small ones can cripple the best-laid plans. According to a report by the Securities and Exchange Commission, "A 1 percent increase in a fund's annual expenses can reduce an investor's ending account balance in that fund by 18 percent after 20 years."

John Waggoner, in a front-page article in *USA Today*, said it this way: "The more you pay your fund or your broker, the less you earn and the less likely you are to have enough to retire."

Warning that financial services companies can nickel-and-dime investors out of huge amounts of money, he gave this example: Earning 7 percent annually, you need to save $820 a month to accumulate $1 million in 30 years. But if you pay out two percentage points a year to funds and brokers, "you'll end up with $828,000—$172,000 short." That $172,000 shortfall amounts to more than 17 years of the $820 monthly payments that you made—and that money is just gone.

Two percentage points might seem like an uncommonly large leak. But Morningstar Inc. reports the expense ratios for thousands of mutual funds, individually and by categories. In Morningstar's nine broad style-box categories for mutual funds, such as large-cap growth, mid-cap blend, and small-cap value, average annual expense ratios in January 2005 ranged from a low of 1.27 percent (large blend) to a high of 1.71 percent (small growth). The average of the nine category averages was 1.52 percent. Those numbers represent fees charged directly to investors by mutual funds.

When those funds are held in nonretirement (taxable) accounts, Uncle Sam takes a cut almost every year, too. Morningstar computes an average annual tax cost for each mutual fund it tracks. (This is the tax cost of owning the fund and assumes that you don't sell any shares.)

The average annual tax cost of the 25 largest diversified U.S. equity funds over the 10 years ending in mid-2004 was 1.34 percent. The average expense ratio of these 25 funds was 0.69 percent, for a total leak of 2.03 percentage points per year. And that is for a group of funds with below-average expenses.

Those expense ratios don't include the cost of heavy portfolio turnover. Many investors in the late 1990s were enamored of technology funds, which have portfolio turnover averaging 254 percent per year. That heavy trading drives up costs (driving down returns). Obviously, investment managers and salespeople deserve to be paid, and investors should expect to pay for legitimate expenses. Taxes also must be paid. But if you overpay, you erode your returns and give back money that rightly should belong to you.

Investors leave money on the table in many ways. They invest in tax-inefficient funds. They trade too often. They fail to take full advantage of tax-sheltered accounts such as IRAs and 401(k)s. The Internal Revenue Service reports that in 2000, fewer than 10 percent of the taxpayers who were eligible to contribute to an IRA did so. Those who use tax shelters often invest in the wrong assets.

Investors overpay their taxes because they keep poor records and thus pay taxes twice on the same income when they finally sell. The same thing happens when they invest in mutual funds immediately before taxable distributions, thus being taxed on part of their own investments. On the expense side, investors who don't know or don't care pay more than they need to for sales commissions, recurring expenses, and trading costs.

Many investors constantly seek higher returns, which are often available to those who take higher risks. But there's a risk-free way to achieve higher returns, and that's to limit the erosion of taxes and expenses. This chapter shows how to do that.

This is a chapter the investment industry hopes you'll skip over quickly.

There are many things beyond investors' control. But expenses and taxes are two of the most important exceptions. If you pay careful attention to this topic, you will benefit. If you neglect it, you will pay for your negligence. It's as simple as that.

Let's tackle expenses first, then taxes. There are three major areas of expenses for investors: sales expenses, operating expenses, and trading costs.

Trading costs are just that: the expense any investor has in buying and selling stocks, bonds, and other securities. In mutual funds, trading costs are usually neither explicitly disclosed nor subject to much control by fund shareholders. The best way to keep these costs under control is to seek low-turnover mutual funds such as index funds.

At or near the opposite end of the scale are technology funds, which as a group have average annual portfolio turnover of 254 percent. Aside from the costs of all that trading, think for a second what that figure means to investors. If you buy a technology fund, you might think you are hiring a manager to make smart long-term choices of the most promising companies and technological advances. But 254 percent annual turnover suggests that these managers are mostly engaged in frantically chasing short-term trends.

Investors can do much more about recurring expenses and selling expenses—but only if they take a proactive role. To the greatest extent possible, Wall Street likes to mask expenses and redirect investors' attention elsewhere. To manage your expenses effectively, you'll have to first be able to recognize them, then make the choice—when you have it—to accept them, limit them, or eliminate them.

Almost all investors pay ongoing management expenses. These include all the normal costs to run a fund and support existing shareholders: accountants, custodians, lawyers, transfer agents, an annual meeting, administration, salaries, rent, printing, statements, taxes, regulatory compliance, and so forth.

Mutual funds' recurring expenses are relatively easy to identify. Every mutual fund must specify how much it charges investors on an annual basis. For example, the giant Fidelity Magellan Fund's expense ratio is 0.7 percent per year. The popular Legg Mason Value Primary Fund, run by legendary manager Bill Miller, charges more than twice as much: 1.7 percent. This is a leak.

Both Magellan and Legg Mason Value are classified by Morningstar as large blend funds. Frugal investors who choose index funds can get access to the same asset class for 0.1 percent at Fidelity or 0.18 percent at Vanguard.

Sometimes Magellan and Legg Mason Value outperform the indexes, but that extra performance is not reliable. However, the higher expenses they charge investors are quite reliable. Advice: when you can, stack the odds in your favor by using low-cost index funds.

You may think money market funds are generic products, easily interchangeable. But acting on that assumption could be costly. Morningstar studied some of the largest taxable money market funds and found that five of them—Schwab, Fidelity, Vanguard, Putnam, and Alliance—had almost identical performance before expenses. After expenses, their yields ranged from 0.57 percent for Alliance Bernstein Capital Reserves to 1.27 percent for Vanguard Prime Money Market.

Table 11.1 shows the difference. The Vanguard fund kept 20 percent of the portfolio's return for itself, giving shareholders 80 cents on the dollar. The Alliance Bernstein fund kept 63 percent for itself, leaving only 37 cents on the dollar for its shareholders. This is a leak.

Funds aren't alone in charging regular fees. Most investors with accounts smaller than $50,000 at Charles Schwab & Co. are charged a maintenance fee of $30 per quarter, or $120 a year. On a $10,000 account, that's 1.2 percent. Many other brokerages charge more than that. This is a leak.

Investors usually have a choice about the brokerage house they deal with. But that's not the case with employees who are

Table 11.1

Anatomy of Two Money Market Funds

Fund	Return before expenses	Expenses	Yield to investors	Percentage of return lost to expenses
Alliance Bernstein Capital Reserves	1.55%	0.98%	0.57%	63%
Vanguard Prime Money Market	1.59%	0.32%	1.27%	20%

charged up to 2 percent a year for the costs of administering their companies' 401(k) plans—in addition, of course, to regular mutual fund fees. This is a leak.

Most mutual fund companies and other financial institutions charge annual maintenance fees of $10 or more for IRA accounts. That fee is often waived for larger accounts, but investors who don't consolidate their IRAs can easily pay $100 a year this way. This is a leak.

Variable annuities are notorious, often charging expenses that total more than 2.5 percentage points. In addition, investors in annuities often must pay an annual contract fee of $30 to $50. Some annuity accounts charge a fee every time an investor swaps between investments within the plan. (About half of all investors in annuities wind up paying surrender charges for cashing out before a minimum contract period that can be 10 years or more.) These are leaks.

Each one of these leaks may seem small by itself. Wall Street likes it that way. (How much time and energy will somebody spend to avoid a $10 annual IRA fee?) Expenses are usually disclosed in writing, but they are rarely emphasized. And investors often get the disclosure only after they have committed their money.

The cure? Remember that investment firms are not charities. If you don't see an expense disclosure, ask somebody to point it out to you. Always seek less expensive ways to achieve what you need. Always ask about expenses. When you hear a pitch about some great product or program, you should be more interested in how much it costs than in how much a salesperson thinks it will return.

Sales costs also are largely within investors' control. These include brokerage commissions, sales loads on mutual fund purchases, and extraordinary expense ratios charged to owners of some classes of fund shares. I could easily write a book on this topic alone, but for now, part of a chapter will have to do. Since I'm recommending mutual funds, I'll concentrate on their sales costs.

To oversimplify the case slightly, mutual funds essentially come in two flavors: load funds and no-load funds. In this context, when you see the word "load," think "sales commission."

When you invest $10,000 in a no-load fund, the entire $10,000 is invested on your behalf and goes to work for you. Because there's no sales commission, you won't find out about these funds from brokers or financial advisers who are compensated only by sales commissions. You must find these funds yourself (or pay an adviser to find them for you) and make your own decisions about them. Doing it yourself—with the help you'll find in this book—is an easy way to effectively add hundreds or even thousands of dollars to your nest egg.

In a load fund, a sales commission is subtracted from your investment. Invest $10,000 in a fund with a 5.75 percent front-end load (this is a usual arrangement for class A shares), and only $9,425 is invested for you. That's what your account will be worth at the end of the first day you own the fund.

The debate over the merits of load funds and no-load ones can be fierce. I'm going to give you my point of view, and I'll back up every bit of it. You'll find other points of view strongly held by people who sell funds, and by some of their customers. In the end, you'll have to make up your own mind.

I can't see any reason most well-informed investors should pay a sales commission to buy a fund. Certainly anybody who is capable of understanding this book can recognize and find good funds without paying for that service from a broker whose interests are almost certainly in conflict with those of the investor.

In 1995 I wrote an article (available on the web site for this book) called "Ten Reasons Why You Should Never Buy a Load Fund." I'd like to discuss some of those points here.

I don't know how to say it any more bluntly than this: Sales loads don't do you any good. (In fact, they do the opposite, as we shall see.)

A mutual fund is really just a pool of money being managed to accomplish some purpose. The load is money paid to the salesperson who brings in the money. The commission doesn't help compensate the portfolio manager. The commission simply diverts money away from that manager by reducing the potential assets under management. (Your full $10,000 could be in the fund instead of only $9,425.) This is a leak.

Every study I've ever seen concludes that over long periods of time there is no statistically significant difference in the returns of all load funds and all no-load funds—assuming that you ignore the load. But ignoring the load or sales commission is silly, because it makes a big difference, one that grows over time. Paying a load puts load fund investors at an immediate disadvantage, because they must start out with less money for every dollar out of their pockets.

The mathematics are simple, and you can figure them yourself with a calculator. Imagine two funds with identical portfolio performance. One charges you a 5.75 percent front-end load, the other is no-load. Result: You will always have 6.1 percent more money in the no-load account than in the load account. (That figure represents the sales load when it is properly computed as a percentage of the amount actually invested. On a $10,000 investment, the $575 load is 6.1 percent of the $9,425 that is invested in the fund.) With a $10,000 investment in two funds that earn 10 percent annually, the difference after 15 years is $2,401. The load fund account has an ending balance of $39,371, versus $41,772 in the no-load fund.

Not all load funds have up-front sales commissions. Class B shares of load funds (sometimes incorrectly described by salespeople as "no-load") charge pointedly higher expense ratios instead of up-front sales loads. This robs performance as well.

Typically, class B shares charge a declining back-end load to investors who fail to leave their money in long enough for the extra expenses to cover the sales commission that wasn't collected up front. After a stipulated period, often seven years, class B shares convert to class A, and from that point their expense ratios decline, improving performance.

For an example, consider the venerable Columbia Acorn Fund. Its no-load shares (now closed to new investors) have an expense ratio of 0.81 percent. Its class A shares charge 1.2 percent and its class B shares charge 1.95 percent. All three share classes have the same underlying portfolio.

To continue the example above, assume that the underlying portfolio earns 10 percent per year, after the 0.81 percent expenses of the no-load shares. After 15 years, an investor in the no-load shares would have an account worth $41,772. An investor in the class B shares, on the other hand, would get a lower return for the first seven years, 8.85 percent to be exact, reflecting the higher expense ratio. Starting in the eighth year, after the original shares converted to class A shares, the expense ratio would decline and annual performance would increase to 9.61 percent.

After 15 years, the investor in class B shares would have an account worth $37,722. That's $4,050 less than in the no-load fund with exactly the same portfolio and the same manager. That difference is more than 40 percent of the investor's initial $10,000 investment, and it's entirely the result of the sales commission, which in class B shares is taken out a little bit at a time for as long as the investor owns those shares.

Tens of thousands of investors pay these sales loads, whether they are hidden or disclosed, every year. The interesting question is whether they receive anything in return. Presumably such fees buy the advantage of having a salesperson choose funds.

But I don't believe it happens. I've seen thousands of investors' portfolios over the years, and I've had no choice but to conclude that investors in load funds don't get good asset allocation advice. Instead, what they get in most cases is a collection of funds that are easy to sell—primarily large-cap U.S. growth funds.

For long-term investors, loads are much higher than they seem. If you could avoid paying a $1,000 sales charge by investing in a no-load fund, and assuming the fund you bought and the fund you didn't buy each compounded at 10 percent, in 25 years you would wind up with nearly $11,000 more. In effect, the $1,000 load cost you $11,000. This is not a small leak. It's a huge leak.

Even when you pay a sales commission, you might not get what you think you are buying. Some fund salespeople say they earn their commissions by finding funds with the best managers. But what happens if, shortly after you buy into such a fund, the manager leaves to run some other fund? At best, you have paid for the track record of a manager who's not working for you. At worst, if you decide to follow that manager to a new load fund, you might wind up paying a second sales commission. Next time you're considering investing in any fund because of its manager, remember this: The best managers are the ones who get new job offers.

Many investors in actively managed mutual funds, no doubt encouraged by advisers who earn commissions by selling them, apparently believe that all my hand-wringing about expenses is irrelevant when a particular fund achieves a superior return. On the surface, it would seem that investors need not care about expenses as long as a fund's return is satisfactory. That's because the fund's expense ratio is already taken into account when the return is calculated.

If a high expense ratio normally brought a premium return that investors could count on, then paying those higher expenses would be a rational choice. (Millions of investors must wish that smart investing were that simple!) However, every rigorous study that I'm familiar with on mutual fund performance shows exactly the same thing: Paying above-average expenses makes above-average performance less likely, not more likely. The reason is simple: Expenses don't enhance performance. They erode it. Every $1 you unnecessarily pay or lose now costs you not only that $1 but also the amount that $1 could earn over your remaining lifetime.

I guarantee you that the companies and people who provide financial services have all thought very carefully about how much to charge for those services. Investors who are casual about this subject are only hurting themselves.

Now let's tackle taxes. Entire libraries could be filled with tax information relevant to investors, but in real life, few people have the time or interest to pursue this topic at length. Here I want to hit some topics that relate to mutual fund investors. Please note at the start of this discussion that some of these points do not apply within tax-sheltered accounts such as IRAs and 401(k) plans.

Mutual funds with high portfolio turnover generate higher tax burdens than funds with lower turnover. The introduction to this chapter mentioned the annual tax cost (1.1 percentage points) of 25 of the largest U.S. equity funds.

Even though most investors have their income and capital gains distributions reinvested, taxes must be paid on those distributions. Some fund managers care more about those taxes than others.

Setting aside continuing expenses, consider the two largest mutual funds in the United States, the Vanguard 500 Index and Fidelity Magellan, both of which are dominated by giant growth stocks (Table 11.2). These two funds are listed in the table, along with Morningstar's calculation of their annual tax loss in the 10 years ending in December 2004. This loss is the percentage of their holdings that each fund's shareholders who were in the highest tax brackets would have paid in taxes year by year as a result of income and capital gains distributions. Think of the tax loss figure as a leak, a drag on performance.

For investors in taxable accounts, the combined annual ex-

Table 11.2

Tax Losses of Largest U.S. Equity Funds

Fund	Annual tax loss
Fidelity Magellan (FMAGX)	1.47%
Vanguard 500 Index (VFINX)	0.61%

pense and tax loss ratios add up to 2.17 percent for Magellan versus 0.79 percent for 500 Index. Which would you rather own? Investors who take the trouble to find such information wind up with much more efficient portfolios. Those who don't bother wind up with big leaks.

Casual or sloppy fund investors sometimes pay taxes twice on the same income. Remember those capital gains and income distributions? I hope so, because the chances are that you reinvested them in more fund shares. That makes those amounts part of the tax basis of your investment in the fund. If you fail to increase your basis accordingly, you'll report (and pay taxes on) larger gains (or smaller losses) than you actually have.

The solution is to keep good annual records so you know how much you paid for the shares you own. At the end of each calendar year, keep your annual fund statements (you can discard the interim statements). Most mutual funds now provide average cost information when you sell. But have your own records as a backup. Investors who sell zero-coupon bonds should also make sure they aren't reporting gains on which they have already paid taxes.

I hope it's obvious that investors pay too much in taxes when they neglect to use IRAs and other retirement accounts for which they are eligible. The Roth IRA is the most tax-efficient vehicle around; if you ignore it you are essentially shooting yourself in the foot.

Many investors ignore the opportunity to invest in tax-managed funds that are run specifically to keep the government's hands out of investors' pockets. We discuss those in the next chapter.

Too many investors pay unnecessary taxes because they incorrectly allocate assets between their taxable and tax-sheltered accounts. The general rule is that as much as possible, tax-efficient assets should go in taxable accounts while tax-inefficient assets belong in tax-sheltered accounts.

Here's what that means: Index equity funds and tax-managed funds belong in taxable (nonsheltered) accounts. Taxable fixed-income funds, real estate funds, and (for investors who own them against my recommendations) actively managed funds and variable annuities (see the box on page 144) all belong in tax-sheltered accounts.

If You Already Own a Load Fund

If you already own one or more load funds, you won't necessarily benefit from selling them. What you should do depends partly on what class of shares you have and how long you have owned them.

If you bought class A shares, the kind with the load charged up front, your money is gone. For practical purposes, you now own a no-load fund—unless you are charged a load for adding new money.

Once you buy class B shares, you are going to pay the full sales commission one way or another. There's no way to get out of it. If you hold the shares a given number of years (often six or seven), you'll pay the load in the form of extraordinarily high expenses for that time, and then the shares will automatically convert to class A shares, which have a lower expense ratio (and correspondingly higher performance). If you sell before the conversion date, you'll pay an exit fee, a back-end load that will effectively finish compensating the fund for the sales commission it paid.

If you own class B shares and you're thinking of selling them, it might make sense to wait until you pass an anniversary date that reduces the exit fee, which typically drops by one percentage point per year that you own the shares. But if that anniversary date is more than half a year away, the wait might not be worthwhile.

If you own class C shares, you'll pay the load in the form of extraordinary expenses for as long as you own the shares. These shares never convert to class A, so the expense ratio never drops. On the other hand, there's usually no exit fee after you have owned these shares for at least a year. In general, the sooner you sell class C shares, the better off you will be.

Whatever class of shares you own, it's not necessarily a good idea to hang onto a load fund. Even if, in the case of class B shares, you own the shares long enough to avoid a withdrawal fee, you may still be in a fund that isn't right for you because of the asset class of its portfolio.

Here's the best advice I can give you: Start with the asset allocation process described in this book and determine the best mix of asset classes for you. Then ask yourself: Does this load fund I own fit neatly in the plan that I should have? Does it have a good record, low expenses, low portfolio turnover, and reputable management? If all the answers are positive, keep the fund.

If you don't have a clear idea why you invested in the fund, or if it doesn't fit into the plan you have made for attaining your objectives, and if it's definitely something you would not invest in again, consider selling in order to find something that will be more suitable for you.

A final consideration concerns taxes. If a sale would result in a taxable capital gain, you'll have to weigh that cost against the cost of continuing to own a fund that you have determined is wrong for you. If the solution to this trade-off isn't obvious, enlist the help of a professional adviser who doesn't sell products (see Chapter 15).

Selling a load fund (or any other investment that you

have determined may have been a mistake) probably won't be at the top of your priority list of things you want to do. It's the sort of move that's easy to put off. But putting it off might cost you thousands of dollars. On the other hand, doing it as soon as you recognize it as a good idea could make you thousands of extra dollars.

You may not be able to segregate all your assets that way. But to the extent you can, that's the division you should make.

I'd like to mention one final tax mistake that mutual fund investors often make: They pay taxes on other people's income and capital gains. How do they accomplish such an astonishing feat? By buying shares soon before income or capital gains distributions. Most parts of the tax code have at least some semblance of being fair. But this one doesn't.

Assume for a moment that you invest $10,000 in a fund and a few days later that fund declares its annual capital gains distribution. After a good year, that distribution could amount to 10 percent of the fund's value, or $1,000 in this hypothetical case. Assuming you have the distribution reinvested in the fund, before taxes you are in exactly the same position that you were before the distribution. You have more shares, but each of them is worth less.

But then along comes Uncle Sam, who says that $1,000 distribution is a capital gain on which you must pay taxes. Even though it was your own money that was paid back to you, the tax law says it's income and subject to tax. If you pay at a 15 percent capital gains rate, this will cost you $150. To pay the tax, you must either sell some of your fund shares or use other money—which is the equivalent of investing more in the fund, without getting more shares.

This is a very annoying leak that you can avoid. Here's how: Before you make a sizeable investment in a mutual fund in the last two months of the year (when most annual capital gains distributions are declared), inquire about upcoming distributions. If you can postpone your purchase until right after the distribution, you'll avoid this tax hit. This isn't difficult. But it's an excellent example of the lesson I hope you take away from this chapter: Investors who pay attention to details are much less likely to be left in the dust. Getting the details right is one of the most reliable ways I know to say goodbye to anxiety and say hello to peace of mind, to wind up with more money along with more time and energy to pursue the other priorities in your life.

Variable Annuities

A variable annuity is a contract between an investor and an insurance company. It allows investments to accumulate on a tax-deferred basis. Variable annuities are terrific if you are producing them (insurance companies) or selling them (insurance agents and other planners). But if you're buying them, they are usually a lethal combination of too-high expenses and too-high taxes.

Variable annuity expenses are notoriously high. Morningstar reported that, late in 2004, the expenses charged by the average domestic stock subaccount (equivalent to a mutual fund) in its variable annuity database were 2.1 percent annually. That was about twice the 1.1 percent charged by the average no-load mutual fund—and 20 times as much as some index funds.

Part of the charge is for life insurance that most likely will be worthless even as it increases in cost. That sounds harsh, but here's how it works: The insurance premium you pay is calculated each year as a percentage of your total account balance. If the value of your account doubles, your premium will double.

But this insurance typically guarantees only that if you die, your heirs will receive at least as much as you originally invested. As long as your account is worth more than your initial investment, the insurance company won't ever have to pay off. This has to be the most profitable insurance any company can sell. As the company's risk goes down (with every dollar you make), the premiums it collects go up.

Annuities usually require investors who want their money back to pay surrender charges or liquidation penalties for "early" withdrawals, typically in the first 6 to 10 years of the contract. That sacrifices liquidity, the ability to get your money back from an investment when you need it. In addition, the IRS adds penalties for investors who take their money out before age 59½.

While most variable annuities offer several investment options, usually the asset classes available are quite limited, and most are actively managed funds. This means it's impossible for investors to make their money work very hard.

It's ironic that variable annuities are promoted as tax shelters. If most people understood the details, they'd never invest. There are three main tax flaws with variable annuities:

- Money you put into them isn't tax-deductible.

- All earnings in the account are eventually taxed as ordinary income at the investor's highest tax bracket. When you buy a variable annuity, you say goodbye to the benefits of the 15 percent cap on tax rates for dividends and capital gains. The tax rate you pay can be more than twice that high.

- Even though you may have a substantial tax basis in the account, when you start living off your annuity savings, all your withdrawals will be considered income (on which you must pay tax at your top rate) until you've used up 100 percent of your earnings.

Only then will you be able to withdraw your original investment tax-free. By that time, you're likely to feel that you've been taxed to the max.

Here's my bottom-line advice on variable annuities: Don't buy one unless you have read the entire contract and you're sure you understand every paragraph. Furthermore, if any insurance agent or adviser tells you to put a variable annuity inside an IRA or other tax shelter, immediately terminate the conversation.

If you already own a variable annuity, or if you decide you are one of the exceptions for whom a variable annuity is the right product, do what's known as a Section 1035 exchange and move the assets into a low-cost, no-commission annuity from Vanguard or Dimensional Fund Advisors, where you at least won't be hemmed in by stiff early redemption penalties.

For a more complete discussion of this topic, see the article "All About Annuities" at www.wiley.com/go/paul merriman.

Chapter TWELVE

Putting Your Perfect Portfolio to Work

Genius is the ability to put into effect what is in your mind.

—F. Scott Fitzgerald

If you have followed the sequence of learning and thinking and evaluating the steps in the book so far, by this time you know what kinds of assets are likely to maximize your chances of investment success while keeping your risk under control. The question at this point is purely practical: Where is the very best place to put your money so you get what you need?

You know you should use no-load mutual funds to diversify widely. You know you should keep your expenses low and your taxes low whenever you can. There are many places you can invest your money to get an adequate return.

But there's no reason you should settle for an OK portfolio when you can have a great one.

This chapter shows you seven ways to go from OK to great. None of them is perfect, but any one of them can be a low-cost ticket to tax-efficient investing that will do what you need.

Exchange-traded funds (ETFs) have no minimum balance requirements, letting you invest in pools of assets with small amounts of money. Their main shortcoming is the lack of access to some important asset classes.

A number of no-load mutual fund families offer low-cost funds that are definitely a cut above the ordinary. For investors with 401(k) plans run by Schwab, T. Rowe Price, Fidelity, or Vanguard—and for other investors who for whatever reason want to keep their money at one of those companies—our suggested portfolios show how to take maximum advantage of that opportunity.

For taxable accounts, there are excellent funds specifically managed to reduce the income tax bite, preserving more of the portfolios' growth and income for shareholders instead of letting Uncle Sam nibble away at them.

None of those portfolios includes every important asset class. For do-it-yourself investors who don't mind using multiple fund families and some actively managed funds in their portfolios, we offer a go-anywhere "model portfolio" that does represent every asset class investors need.

If you want the very best assets at the lowest cost and with the highest tax efficiency, check out the "ultimate equity portfolio" of funds from Dimensional Fund Advisors (DFA). These funds are off-limits to do-it-yourself investors—they are available only through investment advisers. Some people regard that as a drawback, because investment advisers charge management fees and have account size minimums. However, as you will see in Chapter 14, there is much value in having an adviser.

In some ways, this is the most daunting chapter in this book, because it's full of tables and comparisons of many kinds. Here's a quick guide to the parts that might be of immediate interest:

- If you're enrolled in a 401(k) plan run by T. Rowe Price, you'll find our recommendations in Table 12.2.

- If your 401(k) or other account is at Fidelity, our recommendations are in Table 12.3.

- Vanguard investors will find our recommendations in Table 12.4.

- Investors at Schwab will find our recommendations in Table 12.5.

- To see how to build a portfolio of the best no-load funds available anywhere, turn to the Merriman model portfolio in Table 12.6.

- You'll find what we consider the very best of the very best in Table 12.7, the ultimate equity portfolio.

- On the web site for this book you will find suggested portfolios for retirement plans that use TIAA-CREF and other fund families, as well as our specific recommendations for 401(k) plans run by large employers such as the federal government, Boeing, IBM, and Microsoft.

Most investors, for various reasons, wind up with portfolios that almost by default are heavily overweighted in large U.S. growth stocks. Historically, this asset class has had the lowest long-term performance since 1926 of all those we recommend.

As you know from earlier chapters in this book, investors who want to make their money work hard for them must go far beyond the most popular funds. Fortunately, there are a number of ways to do this.

Exchange traded funds, because they don't have minimum initial investment requirements, give small investors a super-low-cost way to gain access to many asset classes. Most are based on stock indexes, making them tax efficient and exempt from the costs (and likely underperformance) of active management.

As their name implies, these funds are traded on stock exchanges, most often the American Stock Exchange. They can be bought and sold any time during market hours, at whatever the market price is at any moment. (By contrast, mutual funds can be bought only once a day and they have only one price, set at the market's close.) ETFs also can be sold short or purchased on margin.

These attributes make ETFs convenient for traders, but they don't offer any particular advantage to long-term investors. One important downside of ETFs is that they can't be bought or sold without paying a brokerage commission. This commission is usually a small number of dollars, and for large purchases it amounts to a tiny fraction of the purchase or sales price. However, the sales commission can be a deterrent to periodic rebalancing, an important step in keeping risks under control.

The other main drawback to ETFs is that they aren't available in all the asset classes that investors need. The ETF suggested portfolio (Table 12.1) doesn't have representation in international value, international small-cap, or international small-value stocks. Those are serious omissions that make ETFs an imperfect way to diversify.

To add a fixed-income component to this portfolio, use equal

Table 12.1

Exchange-Traded Funds Suggested Portfolio (all equity)

Fund	Asset class	Percentage	Ticker
S&P Depository Receipts	U.S. large-cap blend	12.5	SPY
I-Shares Russell 1000 Value	U.S. large-cap value	12.5	IWD
I-Shares Russell 2000 Index	U.S. small-cap blend	12.5	IWM
I-Shares Russell 2000 Value	U.S. small-value	12.5	IWN
I-Shares MSCI EAFE	International large-cap	40	EFA
I-Shares MSCI Emerging Markets	Emerging markets	10	EEM

parts of the I-Shares Lehman 1–3 year fund (SHY) and the I-Shares Lehman Aggregate Bond (AGG). Multiply the percentages in the table by the equity portion of the overall portfolio. For example, for a 60 percent equity portfolio, multiply each percentage by 0.6. (That would give you 6 percent in emerging markets, for one example.)

This and every other suggested portfolio in this chapter are available online at www.wiley.com/go/paulmerriman. They will be updated there whenever our recommendations change.

T. Rowe Price is a venerable and respected no-load fund family known for conservative management, wide diversification, and reasonable expenses. You won't often find these funds at the very top of performance lists, but you'll almost never find them near the bottom, either. Nor will you find gimmick funds here. T. Rowe Price by and large stays with the tried and true.

Two of the funds listed in Table 12.2, our T. Rowe Price suggested portfolio (small-cap stock and small-cap value), are closed to new investors. However, they are available to many investors in T. Rowe Price 401(k) plans.

To add a fixed-income component to the T. Rowe Price portfolio, put 50 percent of the fixed-income portion into the T. Rowe Price Short-Term Bond Fund (PRWBX) and 25 percent each into

Table 12.2

T. Rowe Price Suggested Portfolio (all equity)

Fund (all are T. Rowe Price)	Asset class	Percentage	Ticker
Equity Index 500	U.S. large-cap blend	12.5	PREIX
Value	U.S. large-cap value	12.5	TRVLX
Small-Cap Stock	U.S. small-cap blend	12.5	OTCFX
Small-Cap Value	U.S. small-cap value	12.5	PRSVX
International Equity Index	International large-cap	10	PIEQX
International Growth & Income	International large-cap value	10	TRIGX
International Discovery	International small-cap	20	PRIDX
Emerging Market Stock	Emerging markets	10	PRMSX

the T. Rowe Price U.S. Bond Index Fund (PBDIX) and the T. Rowe Price International Bond Fund (RPIBX). Multiply the percentages in the table by the equity portion of the overall portfolio. For example, for a 60 percent equity portfolio, multiply each percentage by 0.6. (That would give you 9 percent in Equity Index 500, for one example.) Unfortunately, investors at T. Rowe Price must do without a very important asset class, international small-cap value stocks.

Fidelity is the powerhouse of 401(k) plans, and millions of employees depend on Fidelity funds for important parts of their retirement savings. Fidelity has a deep, highly respected pool of securities analysts and offers a huge variety of funds with specialized portfolios, most of which investors don't really need. The company does an above-average job of keeping its costs reasonable, offering some index funds with extremely low expense ratios.

However, many of the 401(k) plans put together by Fidelity are dominated by the company's large-cap U.S. funds, depriving many investors of access to funds [e.g., international small-cap

(FISMX)] in asset classes that could enhance their diversification. Table 12.3 shows our Fidelity suggested portfolio.

To add a fixed-income component to the Fidelity portfolio, split the fixed-income assets equally between the Fidelity Short-Term Bond Fund (FSHBX) and the Fidelity Intermediate Bond Fund (FTHRX). Multiply the percentages in the table by the equity portion of the overall portfolio. For example, for a 60 percent equity portfolio, multiply each percentage by 0.6. (That would give you 7.5 percent in the Spartan 500 Index Fund, for example.) The Fidelity portfolio suffers from the same weakness as the T. Rowe Price lineup: There's no access to small-cap value stocks, either in the United States or internationally.

For many years we favored the low-cost, tax-efficient index funds of Vanguard for do-it-yourself investors. Unfortunately, Vanguard in 2004 closed its International Explorer Fund (VINEX) to new accounts, locking new investors out of two important asset classes, international small-cap and international small-value stocks. Table 12.4 shows our Fidelity suggested portfolio.

To add a fixed-income component to the Vanguard portfolio, split the fixed-income assets equally between the Vanguard Short-Term Investment Grade Fund (VFSTX) and the Vanguard Total Bond Market Index Fund (VBMFX). Multiply the percent-

Table 12.3

Fidelity Suggested Portfolio (all equity)

Fund (Fidelity)	Asset class	Percentage	Ticker
Spartan 500 Index	U.S. large-cap blend	12.5	FSMKX
Equity Income	U.S. large-cap value	12.5	FEQIX
Small-Cap Stock	U.S. small-cap blend	25	FSLCX
Spartan International Index	International large-cap	40	FSIIX
Emerging Markets	Emerging markets	10	FEMKX

Table 12.4

Vanguard Suggested Portfolio (all equity)

Fund (Vanguard)	Asset class	Percentage	Ticker
500 Index	U.S. large-cap blend	12.5	VFINX
Value Index	U.S. large-cap value	12.5	VIVAX
Small-Cap Index	U.S. small-cap blend	12.5	NAESX
Small-Cap Value Index	U.S. small-cap value	12.5	VISVX
Developed Markets Index	International large-cap	20	VDMIX
International Value	International large-cap value	20	VTRIX
Emerging Markets Index	Emerging markets	10	VEIEX

ages in the table by the equity portion of the overall portfolio. For example, for a 60 percent equity portfolio, multiply each percentage by 0.6. (That would give you 7.5 percent in the Vanguard 500 Index Fund, for example.)

Some investors may wish to use Charles Schwab's brokerage, which offers convenient access to many funds from many families. Our suggested portfolio for Schwab clients (Table 12.5) provides entries in every important asset class we recommend.

To add a fixed-income component to the Schwab portfolio, put half the fixed-income assets in Schwab Short-Term Bond Market (SWBDX) and 25 percent each in Schwab Total Bond Market (SWLBX) and PIMCO Foreign Bond D (PFODX). Multiply the percentages in Table 12.5 by the equity portion of the overall portfolio. For example, for a 60% equity portfolio, multiply each percentage by 0.6. (That would give you 7.5 percent in Schwab 1000, for example.)

Each of the portfolios above is convenient, consisting of funds from a single family that can be held in one account. But none of those portfolios covers all the bases. For investors who don't want to compromise on asset classes, I offer the Merriman model portfolio. This group of no-load funds is the best bet for do-it-

Table 12.5

Charles Schwab Suggested Portfolio (all equity)

Fund	Asset class	Percentage	Ticker
Schwab 1000	U.S. large-cap blend	12.5	SNXFX
Soundshore Fund	U.S. large-cap value	12.5	SSHFX
Schwab Small-Cap Index	U.S. small-cap blend	12.5	SWSMX
Heartland Value Plus	U.S. small-cap value	12.5	HRVIX
Schwab International Index	International large-cap	10	SWINX
Causeway International Value	International large-cap value	10	CIVVX
Wasatch International Growth	International small-cap growth	10	WAIGX
Third Avenue International Value	International small-cap value	10	TAVIX
American Century Emerging Markets	Emerging markets	10	TWMIX

yourself investors who are willing to go anywhere and who can accept the inconvenience of multiple fund families and multiple statements. Many of these funds may be available through Schwab and other discount brokerages, so it may not be necessary to have as many accounts as this list would suggest.

This portfolio (Table 12.6) is subject to change from time to time as funds close their doors to new investors and new funds appear that may have more attractive features. We keep this model portfolio updated on the web site for this book.

Only three of those nine funds are actively managed, and the portfolio consists of funds from only three families. All charge expenses that range from extremely low (Fidelity's index funds) to reasonably low (the international small-cap and emerging markets funds). To add a fixed-income component, split that part of the portfolio equally between the Vanguard Short-Term

Table 12.6

Merriman Model Portfolio (all equity)

Fund	Asset class	Percentage	Ticker
Fidelity Spartan 500 Index	U.S. large-cap blend	12.5	FSMKX
Vanguard Value Index	U.S. large-cap value	12.5	VIVAX
Vanguard Small-Cap Index	U.S. small-cap blend	12.5	NAESX
Vanguard Small-Cap Value Index	U.S. small-cap value	12.5	VISVX
Fidelity Spartan International Index	International large-cap blend	10	FSIIX
Vanguard International Value	International large-cap value	10	VTRIX
Laudus Rosenberg International Small-Cap	International small-cap	10	RISIX
Third Avenue International Value	International small-cap value	10	TAVIX
Vanguard Emerging Markets Index	Emerging markets	10	VEIEX

Investment Grade Fund and the Vanguard Total Bond Market Index Fund. This will give you the right combination of stability and yield.

Of all the portfolios we've outlined, the last one is the best way I know of for you to build Your Perfect Portfolio using low-cost, tax-efficient, no-load funds available to the public. If you own a portfolio like that and rebalance it each year, adding money as you can, you will probably be among the most successful long-term investors.

However, I'm committed to giving you the very best possible advice, and that compels me to introduce what I call "the best mutual funds in the world." That's not a description I would ever use casually, but I believe it's true. If you are investing money for a long time, you should find a great spot for it, not just a good spot.

In more than two decades of managing money for clients, the best way I've ever found to build a portfolio is using the no-load asset-class funds offered by Dimensional Fund Advisors (DFA). These funds were specifically created to help investors pinpoint the most productive types of assets, as identified by the academic research that underlies Your Perfect Portfolio.

Dimensional Fund Advisors funds have a couple of drawbacks. First, they are available only through investment advisers, whose management fees are normally around 1 percent annually. Second, advisers who offer these funds normally have minimum account sizes of $100,000 or more. But for investors who can get past those hurdles, I believe DFA funds will provide the extra edge over time that will make them great investments instead of just good ones.

Without further ado, I want to introduce you to the equity part of what I consider the ultimate portfolio (Table 12.7).

As a portfolio, I'll put this combination up against any similarly weighted funds in the same asset classes. It's hard to do a

Table 12.7

The Ultimate Equity Portfolio (all equity)

Fund (Dimensional Fund Advisors)	Asset class	Percentage	Ticker
Large Company	U.S. large-cap blend	12.5	DFLCX
Large Company Value	U.S. large-cap value	12.5	DFLVX
U.S. Micro-Cap	U.S. small-cap blend	12.5	DFSCX
Small Value	U.S. small-cap value	12.5	DFSVX
International Large Company	International large-cap blend	10	DFALX
International Value	International large-cap value	10	DFIVX
International Small	International small-cap	10	DFISX
International Small Value	International small-cap value	10	DISVX
Emerging Markets	Emerging markets	10	DFEMX

long-term comparison against the Merriman model portfolio (Table 12.6), because the Third Avenue International Value Fund has a history only as far back as the start of 2002.

However, the period from the start of 2002 through the end of 2004 encompasses a very unfavorable year (2002), a very favorable year (2003), and a fairly typical market year (2004). As such, it includes market conditions that are different enough to give some idea of how DFA funds stack up to the very best we can find anywhere else. You'll see the comparison in Table 12.8. (Results of the ultimate equity portfolio reported in this chapter are calculated before the effect of any management fee.)

The two portfolios' results for each individual year are not terribly different. But the cumulative effect really adds up. On a $10,000 initial investment made at the start of 2002, this is the difference between having $14,931 or $16,670 after 36 months. That difference, $1,739, is 17 percent of the initial $10,000 investment.

It's also interesting to compare the ultimate equity portfolio with our Vanguard suggested portfolio. We can make that comparison back to 1999, when the Vanguard U.S. Small-Cap Value Fund came on the scene.

In Table 12.9 you'll see year-by-year results for three portfolios. First is the Vanguard suggested portfolio detailed above. It does not include the Vanguard International Explorer Fund and thus has no representation in international small-cap stocks. The second portfolio in Table 12.8 represents our previous Vanguard

Table 12.8

Merriman Model Portfolio versus Ultimate Equity Portfolio, 2002–2004

Portfolio	2002	2003	2004	Cumulative
Merriman Model Portfolio	−15.0%	45.2%	21.0%	49.3%
Ultimate Equity Portfolio	−10.0%	50.1%	23.4%	66.7%

Table 12.9

Vanguard Portfolios versus Ultimate Equity Portfolio, 1999–2004

Portfolio	1999	2000	2001	2002	2003	2004	Cumulative
Vanguard Suggested Portfolio	24.1%	–5.0%	–8.4%	–16.2%	39.8%	19.3%	50.9%
Vanguard with International Explorer	32.7%	–4.0%	–9.0%	–16.1%	42.1%	20.9%	67.1%
Ultimate Equity Portfolio	24.2%	–4.4%	–1.2%	–10.0%	50.1%	23.4%	95.6%

recommendations. It is the same as the Vanguard suggested portfolio (Table 12.4) except for percentages in three international funds: The Vanguard Developed Markets Index Fund and the Vanguard International Value Fund each have 13.3 percent allocations, and the Vanguard International Explorer Fund has a 13.4 percent allocation. The third portfolio is the ultimate equity portfolio (Table 12.7).

The comparison between the two Vanguard groups of funds is a good illustration of what international small-cap stocks can do for a diversified portfolio. The only difference between those two portfolios is the way that 13.4 percent of the assets were invested. On a $10,000 initial investment at the start of 1999, this is the difference between having $15,090 (Vanguard without international small-cap exposure) or having $16,710 (with international small-cap exposure).

As you can see, the ultimate equity portfolio of DFA funds did much better. The critical question is why—and whether that advantage is something investors can reasonably expect in the future.

Dimensional Fund Advisors' superior performance is not the result of better managers picking better stocks. Stock picking plays only a very minor role in these funds, which are passively managed. DFA funds' edge comes from precise asset allocations that give investors more of what they need and less of what they don't need.

To show this, let's compare Vanguard's large-cap U.S. value fund (Vanguard Value Index Fund) with DFA's comparable fund (DFA Large Company Value Fund). Statistically, the DFA fund has a much stronger concentration of value.

Imagine that growth versus value is represented by a straight line across a page, with "pure" value at the far left and "pure" growth at the far right. Statistically, we can measure the orientation along this line for a mutual fund portfolio. Most funds fall somewhere on the line between the extremes of growth and value.

I don't believe investors need to analyze individual stocks, but in order to understand value, I invite you into the following discussion. Most experts on asset allocation look at growth versus value in two ways. First, they consider that low price-earnings (P/E) ratios represent value and high P/E ratios represent growth. Second (regarded by academics as the best measure) is the price-book (P/B) ratio of a stock. This indicates how much investors are willing to pay in relation to a company's book value per share. Book value consists of the cash and all other assets on a company's books, minus all liabilities.

A low P/B ratio suggests that investors place a high importance on physical assets. A high P/B ratio indicates investors think something else is more important, most likely a company's ability to generate future profits. At Microsoft, for example, the company's physical assets and cash hoard are valuable, but they are only incidental in comparison with the brainpower of the company's workforce.

Imagine a company that is facing enormous challenges such as heavy debts, faltering management, and perhaps other serious problems like lawsuits, government crackdowns, or competitors with products that could make this company's products obsolete. In an extreme case, investors might be so unenthusiastic about such a company that the share price could be less than the fire-sale level of the assets in the event that the company was liquidated. That would make it a highly discounted value stock.

If the share price were equal to the book value, for a P/B ratio of 1.0, investors would be saying in effect that the company is worth only the balance sheet value of its buildings, land, trucks, equipment, inventory, cash, and all the other assets on its books, minus the liabilities. That stock price would place no value at all on the company's ability to use those assets to generate profits.

That's an extreme example, and most stocks in value funds are not in terrible trouble, only out of favor for various reasons.

The S&P 500 Index, generally regarded as having a portfolio that represents a midpoint between value and growth, has a P/B ratio of 2.6 as this is being written. (The number goes up and down with stock market cycles, and this figure is always readily accessible at Morningstar.com on the portfolio page for the Vanguard 500 Index Fund.) So for this discussion we can think of a P/B of 2.6 as neutral, representing neither growth nor value.

The portfolio of the DFA Large Company Value Fund has a P/B ratio of 0.9, meaning it is very heavily weighted toward value. Vanguard's Growth Index Fund (VIGRX), by contrast, has a P/B ratio of 3.3.

When you're trying to capture the benefit of investing in value companies, you will get more of that benefit from funds with portfolios of stocks that fall farther to the left (value) side of that imaginary line, companies with lower P/B ratios.

Table 12.10 shows the P/B ratios of the U.S. large-cap value funds in the portfolios we have listed above. As you look at the numbers, remember that the S&P 500 Index's P/B ratio is 2.6. The first three value funds don't stray very far from the broad center, but DFA's portfolio does. In years when value outperforms, that gives DFA a big advantage.

Table 12.11 shows annual (and cumulative) performance for the same four funds for 2001 through 2004.

These numbers reflect only a few years. But the DFA fund's greater orientation to value makes it a much better way to gain the advantage of value investing that we saw in Chapter 8. In Your Perfect Portfolio, value works best when it is clearly differ-

Table 12.10

Price-Book Ratios of U.S. Large-Cap Value Funds

Fund	Price/book ratio	Ticker
T. Rowe Price Value	2.1	TRVLX
Fidelity Equity Income	2.2	FEQIX
Vanguard Value Index	2.2	VIVAX
Dimensional Fund Advisors Large Company Value	1.3	DFLVX

Table 12.11

Performance of U.S. Large-Cap Value Funds

Fund	2001	2002	2003	2004	$10,000 became
T. Rowe Price Value	1.6%	−16.6%	30.0%	15.4%	$12,712
Fidelity Equity Income	−5.0%	−17.2%	30.0%	11.3%	$11,381
Vanguard Value Index	−11.9%	−20.9%	32.3%	15.3%	$10,630
Dimensional Fund Advisors Large Company Value	3.8%	−14.9%	34.4%	18.3%	$14,045

entiated from the overall market. And DFA's fund does that better than any comparable fund I know.

Let's look also at the size factor. To get the full advantage from investing in small-cap companies, you should own really small companies, not just ones at the lower end of the mid-cap category. Again, you can imagine a spectrum from tiny companies with total market capitalization under $50 million to giants like General Electric (over $360 billion). Although there are no hard-and-fast definitions, small-cap stocks are generally regarded as those with market caps of $1.5 billion or less.

Smaller is better, and some funds give investors more "smallness" than others. That's pointedly the case with the DFA U.S. Microcap Fund. In a year when all stocks do well and small-cap stocks do better, the DFA fund should shine. Such a year was 2003. The returns that year for these four funds are shown in Table 12.12; for each fund, I've also included the median market capitalization of its portfolio and the total number of stock holdings.

The DFA size advantage is not an accident. The company's U.S. Microcap Fund invests only in the smallest 20 percent of all U.S. stocks—technically the 9th and 10th deciles based on the size of companies on the New York Stock Exchange.

Table 12.12

Four U.S. Small-Cap Funds, 2003

Fund	2003	Median market capitalization	Stocks in portfolio
T. Rowe Price Diversified Small-Cap Growth	40.2%	$1.382 billion	291
Fidelity Small-Cap Stock	45.0%	$871 million	249
Vanguard Small-Cap Index	45.6%	$1.198 billion	1,748
Dimensional Fund Advisors U.S. Micro-Cap	60.7%	$279 million	2,494

In individual years when smaller stocks are faring worse than average, the effect works in reverse and DFA returns will be hit harder. In 1998, a bad year for small-cap stocks, the DFA U.S. Microcap Fund fell 7.3 percent, compared with a loss of only 2.6 percent for the Vanguard Small-Cap Index Fund.

For the four years 1998 through 2002, $10,000 invested in the Vanguard Small-Cap Index Fund would have shrunk to $9,622; that much invested in the DFA U.S. Microcap Fund would have grown to $12,349.

You can expect the DFA funds that focus on small-cap stocks to underperform when small-cap stocks are lagging large-cap ones. Should that deter you from investing in the DFA funds? I don't think so, and here's why: Over the long term, investors usually receive premium returns for taking carefully controlled risks. Investing in a broadly diversified portfolio of very small companies represents a carefully controlled risk that is likely to give investors a premium return.

So far we have seen two main advantages of DFA funds: They deliver smaller small and more deeply discounted value. DFA funds also excel in a third way. They have low portfolio turnover, which allows them to be more cost efficient and more tax efficient than even index funds.

Funds that track specific indexes must buy and sell periodically whenever the stocks in an index change. The purchases and sales usually coincide with the purchases and sales of every other fund that tracks the same index. It's hard to get the best price when many other big buyers (or sellers) are doing the same thing you are. When an index fund updates its portfolio semiannually, this can cost two to four percentage points of return.

DFA funds are not strictly index funds, and therefore they are not obligated to buy and sell stocks except to keep their portfolios representative of their asset classes. Table 12.13 shows the annual portfolio turnover for 2004 of four funds each in three asset classes from the portfolios above.

In every case, DFA funds had far lower portfolio turnover than the actively managed funds and index funds. This doesn't guarantee higher returns, but it stacks the odds in the investor's favor by plugging a large potential leak.

Investors should focus on what they can control and try not to worry too much about what they can't control. The most important thing investors can control is the kind of assets they put in their portfolios. More than anything else, that determines their returns.

I favor DFA funds because they give investors access to asset classes you can't get anywhere else (e.g., two international small-

Table 12.13

Comparison of Annual Portfolio Turnover in Four Asset Classes

Fund	U.S. large value	U.S. small-cap	International large-cap	Emerging markets
T. Rowe Price	31%	23%	39%	66%
Fidelity	25%	96%	31%	105%
Vanguard	48%	39%	7%	16%
Dimensional Fund Advisors	7%	19%	1%	1%

cap funds versus none at all that are open to new investors at Vanguard), at low cost and with high tax efficiency.

The final moment of truth for serious investors is whether it makes sense to hire an investment adviser in order to get access to DFA funds. For many years I have preached the gospel of low-cost investing. I don't want you to pay a penny more for your investments than you have to. But neither do I want you to be penny wise and pound foolish.

My company's studies indicate that over time, DFA funds should have an advantage of at least one percentage point a year over Vanguard funds, even after the effect of a presumed 1 percent annual management fee. This net advantage can make the difference between retiring when you want to or having to work longer. It can make the difference between running out of money or not. It can make the difference between retiring with a substantial cushion or having to just get by.

Many investors are reluctant to pay for a manager's services. But professional guidance itself can be extremely valuable, as we discuss in Chapter 14. And completely aside from that, if you pay 1 percent of your assets in order to boost them by 2 percent, that could be an excellent investment, with a theoretical return approaching 100 percent.

Tax-Managed Funds

Fidelity's and Vanguard's index funds are extremely tax efficient, as are the asset class funds of DFA. Still, there's another level of tax efficiency that's available to investors in high tax brackets: Both Vanguard and DFA have excellent funds that are specifically managed to minimize the tax leaks from income and capital gains distributions.

What's a tax-managed fund? Two nearly identical Vanguard U.S. large-cap blend funds provide a good example. Table 12.14 is a short table like one we saw in Chapter 11, showing the 10-year annual tax loss for these funds. The index fund is managed without regard to taxes, while the tax-managed one is run in a way designed to minimize taxes that shareholders must pay.

The combination of lower expenses and greater tax efficiency gives the tax-managed fund a small but definitely worthwhile advantage for investors in taxable accounts.

The stocks in these two funds are usually identical or nearly so. But manager Gus Sauter makes trades in the tax-managed fund to realize capital losses in order to offset realized gains. This means the tax-managed fund will sometimes stray slightly from the index. The annualized returns of the tax-managed fund have consistently been slightly higher than those of the index fund—typically about 0.1 percent higher each year. That is without taking taxes into consideration.

When the results are adjusted to reflect taxes that investors in the highest tax brackets would have paid during the 10 years ending December, 2004, the tax-adjusted performance was 11.3 percent for the Vanguard 500 Index Fund and 11.5 percent for the Vanguard Tax-Managed Growth & Income Fund. On a $10,000 investment for 10 years, that's the difference between $29,171 and $29,699. That difference is small, but it's an edge that's reasonably predictable, one more way investors can stack the odds in their favor.

Not every asset class is represented by a tax-managed

Table 12.14

The Effect of Tax Management

Fund	Annual tax loss	Expenses	Total
Vanguard 500 Index (VFINX)	0.61%	0.18%	0.79%
Vanguard Tax Managed Growth & Income (VTGIX)	0.52 %	0.17%	0.69%

Table 12.15

Vanguard Tax-Managed Suggested Portfolio (all equity)

Fund (Vanguard)	Asset class	Percentage	Ticker
Tax-Managed Growth & Income	U.S. large-cap blend	12.5	VTGIX
Value Index	U.S. large-cap value	12.5	VIVAX
Tax-Managed Small-Cap	U.S. small-cap blend	12.5	VTMSX
Small-Cap Value Index	U.S. small-cap value	12.5	VISVX
Tax-Managed International	International large-cap	20	VTMGX
International Value	International large-cap value	20	VTRIX
Emerging Markets Index	Emerging markets	10	VEIEX

fund, but several are. When we design a portfolio for somebody in a high tax bracket, we use our same basic portfolios but substitute tax-managed funds when we can. Table 12.15 shows our Vanguard tax-managed suggested portfolio.

Vanguard's other tax-managed funds include the Tax-Managed Balanced Fund and the Tax-Managed Capital Appreciation Fund. DFA has five tax-managed funds: the DFA Tax-Managed U.S. Equity Fund, the DFA Tax-Managed U.S. Marketwide Value Fund, the DFA Tax-Managed U.S. Small-Cap Fund, the DFA Tax-Managed Small-Cap Value Fund, and the DFA Tax-Managed International Value Fund. Table 12.16 shows how we would modify the ultimate equity portfolio for the most tax-efficient strategy using those funds.

Tax-managed funds don't cover every important asset class, so they can't make up all of a properly diversified portfolio. But adding even a few of them makes a noticeable difference, especially at tax time, when you realize they haven't made any capital gains distributions.

Table 12.16

The Tax-Managed Ultimate Equity Portfolio (all equity)

Fund (Dimensional Fund Advisors)	Asset class	Percentage	Ticker
Tax-Managed U.S. Equity	U.S. large-cap blend	12.5	DTMEX
Tax-Managed Marketwide U.S. Value	U.S. large-cap value	12.5	DTMMX
Tax-Managed U.S. Small-Cap	U.S. small-cap blend	12.5	DFTSX
Tax-Managed U.S. Small-Cap Value	U.S. small-cap value	12.5	DTMVX
International Large Company	International large-cap blend	10	DFALX
Tax-Managed International Value	International large-cap value	10	DTMIX
International Small	International small-cap	10	DFISX
International Small Value	International small-cap value	10	DISVX
Emerging Markets	Emerging markets	10	DFEMX

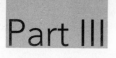

Part III

The Golden Years

Chapter THIRTEEN

Withdrawals: When Your Portfolio Starts Paying You

■■■■■

It is better to live rich than to die rich.

—*Samuel Johnson*

This chapter could be called "The Facts of Life for Retirees." It gets right to the nub of some choices that cannot be avoided. There are very few financial changes as important as retirement. It's the end of paying your portfolio and the start of having your portfolio pay you. How you go about this transition will have financial repercussions for the rest of your life—and most likely for your heirs after you are gone.

You may have saved for many years and invested your money carefully. But when the money has to flow in the reverse direction, suddenly you face four major decisions that will determine the bulk of your financial future.

■ How will you invest your money?

■ How much risk will you take?

■ How much do you need or want regularly from your portfolio?

■ Do you need a fixed income or can you tolerate a variable income?

The first two questions are related, and they're addressed in detail in Part II of this book. We discussed the third question in Chapter 10. I repeat those questions here because the answers may be different for retirees than for preretirees. Thus, those topics may be worth revisiting.

This chapter is concerned with the fourth question and the implications of various possible answers to it.

The biggest financial risk that retirees face is running out of money before they run out of life. How you structure your withdrawals plays a major role in this. This topic is necessarily full of numbers, tables, percentages, projections, and assumptions, all of them very important. But the subject of withdrawals can be emotional and challenging beyond the math. If ever there's a time in a person's financial life when "the rubber finally meets the road," this is it. In a way, this step is a sort of final salary negotiation between retirees and their portfolios.

One of my clients, after I had counseled him and his wife on the subject of how much they were spending, angrily accused me of causing a rift between the two of them. In fact, what I had done was raise issues that he and his wife needed to address early in their retirement. If they hadn't done that, they might have one day faced a crisis and been forced to deal with these issues later, when the stakes were higher and their options much more limited.

This chapter seems to be based on the almost universally shared premise that when it comes to assets and retirement income, more is always better. But I have gone through this process intimately with hundreds of people, and one thing I've seen time and time again is this: Statistically, there doesn't seem to be any inevitable correlation between how much money a retiree has and how happy that retiree is. We have very happy clients who have retired on $30,000 a year—and a few very unhappy ones with six-figure incomes.

Ultimately, having large numbers behind your name in distant computers won't bring you peace, comfort, serenity, or satisfaction. No matter how much or how little money you have, you face the same challenge in retirement: to know where you are, to accept where you are, and to focus on the most important priorities in your life, whatever they are. This chapter will show you how to do that.

I have found that most people reach retirement in one of two situations.

Many investors have enough resources to meet their needs if they use those resources as effectively and productively as possible. These people typically will need to carefully plan and manage their financial affairs to make sure they won't run out of money while they meet their basic needs. For them, "extras" must be rationed thoughtfully.

Many other investors seem to have ample money and, if anything, their "problem" may be overcoming psychological hurdles that make them uncomfortable spending amounts that they could easily afford. (Quite understandably, people in the first camp would be happy to have the "problem" of those with more money than they can ever spend.)

For the first group, the challenge of a withdrawal strategy is to take enough retirement income to cover their basic needs, taking inflation into account, without putting them in danger of running out of money. Because investment returns can't be known in advance, this obviously can be difficult. Sometimes when I counsel people in this situation I encourage them to spend less money than they would like to—or to postpone retirement if they can in order to build up more savings. For the second group, the challenge is to see that they can "loosen up" and use their money in satisfying ways without fear. I often find myself encouraging these retirees to spend more than they want to.

I have seen over the years that most retirees pay too little attention to how they will take money out of their portfolios. It can be tempting, after a lifetime of working and saving, to pay yourself whatever retirement "salary" will make you happy. But unless you have a ton of money or you know you don't have long to live, that can be a big mistake.

The critical question is how much of a portfolio you can or should tap on an annual basis. In Chapter 5, I suggested a ballpark rule of thumb that you should start retirement with savings equal to 20 times the amount you'll need from your portfolio every year. That implies a withdrawal rate of 5 percent.

Most textbooks and many advisers caution against taking out more than 4 to 5 percent of a portfolio annually. I'm certainly in favor of conservative financial management, and if everybody could retire without taking out more than 4 percent per year, I'd be all in favor of it. If you can do that, I'm delighted for you.

However, many people find themselves retired without enough assets to do that. And quite frankly I believe the investment results from Your Perfect Portfolio will be relatively better than those of the more standard portfolios assumed by the experts. If this is true, then that superior performance gives retirees a bit more room to spend what they have saved.

(All these projections and rules of thumb are necessarily based on assumptions. If you invest exclusively in Treasury bills, you certainly can't withdraw even 4 percent every year and still expect your money to last.)

The examples we use with clients, and that I present in my workshops, are typically based on either 6 percent or 8 percent withdrawals. A 6 percent withdrawal rate, which I call "conservative," is typically appropriate for the retiree who must make sure to avoid running out of money. It's generally in tune with meeting the basic target income you were invited to estimate in Chapter 5. The 8 percent rate is more suitable for retirees with more money than they'll ever need. It's aimed at getting them to meet their live-it-up annual income targets.

Before we get into the specifics of how to address the problems of these two groups of retirees, I want to make a few points about the care and nurturing of a retirement portfolio, no matter how much money you have. No rate of withdrawal can be sustained continually from a portfolio that's invested in the wrong assets. That means we must visit asset allocation once again.

As mentioned in Chapter 9 in our discussion of international equity funds, anybody who's regularly withdrawing money from a portfolio must pay attention to more than raw portfolio return figures. Although it might not be intuitively obvious, the details of how that return is achieved can make a huge difference to the long-term success of a portfolio that's supporting withdrawals.

When you're relying on your portfolio for withdrawals, you've got to treat that portfolio with tender loving care by protecting it from losses. This is simple mathematics. Even one terrible year can ruin things for a retiree. Consider a hypothetical retirement scenario that starts with $1 million and a conservative withdrawal strategy of taking out 6 percent ($60,000) the first year and increasing that withdrawal by 3.5 percent to keep up with presumed inflation. As the scheduled withdrawals go up relentlessly every year, they take an increasing bite out of the portfolio. The most important thing we look at in this simulation is not the annualized return of the portfolio. It's the value of the portfolio from year to year. This is the crucial measure of whether a retiree is in any danger of running out of money.

Investors who are accumulating money care most about what they wind up with eventually, and it doesn't matter (at least mathematically) how they get there. If your portfolio lost 45 percent the first year and then enjoyed an unending run of 14 percent annual gains (this is too good to be true in real life, but it makes the point well), you could be happy. In 16 years, you would nearly quadruple your money.

But it might surprise you to know that the very same hypothetical series of returns could spell quick disaster for a retiree making conservative (6 percent) withdrawals. Those returns (after the first year) are very favorable. But when they occur in a $1 million portfolio with gradually increasing withdrawals, they would leave an investor broke after 16 years.

You'll see this in Table 13.1, which shows the first 11 years of results of such a portfolio, which is clearly doomed. Although that example is pure fiction, this sort of thing happens in real life.

Table 13.2 shows year-by-year results of retiring on 6 percent withdrawals as described above, using real returns from two very different asset classes for 1973 through 1985. I didn't choose that period at random. I chose it because during that span of 13

Table 13.1

Hypothetical Retirement Scenario, $1 Million Portfolio

Withdrawal*	Year	Return	Ending value
$60,000	1	−45%	$517,000
$62,100	2	14%	$518,586
$64,274	3	14%	$517,916
$66,523	4	14%	$514,588
$68,851	5	14%	$508,140
$71,261	6	14%	$498,042
$73,755	7	14%	$483,687
$76,337	8	14%	$464,379
$79,009	9	14%	$439,322
$81,774	10	14%	$407,605
$84,636	11	14%	$368,185

Table 13.2

Bond Returns versus Stock Returns, 1973–1985, $1 Million Portfolio

Withdrawal	Year	S&P 500	Ending value	Bonds	Ending value
$60,000	1973	−14.7	$801,820	3.3	$ 971,020
$62,100	1974	−26.5	$543,694	5.9	$ 962,546
$64,274	1975	37.2	$657,765	9.5	$ 983,609
$66,523	1976	23.8	$731,958	12.3	$1,029,887
$68,851	1977	−7.2	$615,363	3.3	$ 992,750
$71,261	1978	6.6	$580,012	2.1	$ 940,840
$73,755	1979	18.4	$599,408	6	$ 919,110
$76,337	1980	32.4	$692,547	6.4	$ 896,711
$79,009	1981	−4.9	$583,475	10.5	$ 903,561
$81,774	1982	21.4	$609,065	26.1	$1,036,273
$84,636	1983	22.5	$642,425	8.6	$1,033,478
$87,598	1984	6.3	$589,781	14.4	$1,082,087
$90,664	1985	32.2	$659,833	18.1	$1,170,870

years, the annualized returns of the S&P 500 Index and the Lehman Brothers Intermediate Government/Corporate Bond Index were nearly identical: 9.6 percent for the S&P 500 Index and 9.5 percent for the bond index. For an investor in the accumulation stage, that gave the stock index a tiny edge over the bond index. Each would have turned an initial $10,000 investment into nearly $33,000.

But for retirees taking increasing withdrawals, the stock returns in those years would have crippled the portfolio. By the end of 1985, the stock portfolio was down to just under $660,000, less than seven times the 1986 scheduled withdrawal. Short of miraculous future returns, this portfolio was clearly doomed after only 13 years. The bond portfolio, which had escaped the heavy stock-market losses of 1973 and 1974, was much healthier.

Out of curiosity, I wondered what would have happened if

this simulation had continued another 20 years, through 2004. That period included one of the great bull markets of the past century, a time when the S&P 500 Index was very productive. Oops! This S&P 500 Index portfolio went broke in 1996, before it could take advantage of the great returns of the late 1990s. From 1973 through 1996, the index had an annualized return of 12.3 percent. This period included 11 calendar years with returns of over 20 percent, six of them over 30 percent. Yet it simply could not keep up, as you see in Table 13.3.

Table 13.3 also shows the bond index, which held up much better even though it had only a 9 percent compound return from 1973 through 1996.

Simplistic retirement projections that use constant returns, even conservative ones, can't do justice to the damage from losing years. In retirement, it's absolutely crucial to find the lowest-risk way to get the return you need. If you keep the risk low enough, you can get along quite nicely with a lower return. That's why a retirement portfolio can almost always benefit from a healthy dose of fixed-income funds. And it's why, as we discussed in Chapter 9, the equity part of a retirement portfolio should include international funds.

One of the themes of this book is that small, incremental changes can have big effects. In my workshops, when I present 10-percent differences in the makeup of a portfolio, I remind the participants that we are talking about owning exactly the same group of stocks, just owning a little more or a little less of them on a percentage basis.

This is what I call fine-tuning your asset allocation.

Now I'd like to show you something dramatic: By shifting 10 percent of the portfolio from bonds to equities (compared with the 50/50 mix in Figure 9.2), we create a portfolio with much greater staying power in the face of escalating 8 percent withdrawals. This is Your Perfect Portfolio at work, with its 60/40 mix of globally diversified equity funds and short-term bond funds.

In Table 13.4, you will see the 50/50 combination—the same

Table 13.3

Bond Returns versus Stock Returns, 1973–1996, $1 Million Portfolio

Withdrawal	Year	S&P 500	Ending value	Bonds	Ending value
$ 60,000	1973	−14.7	$801,820	3.3	$ 971,020
$ 62,100	1974	−26.5	$543,694	5.9	$ 962,546
$ 64,274	1975	37.2	$657,765	9.5	$ 983,609
$ 66,523	1976	23.8	$731,958	12.3	$1,029,887
$ 68,851	1977	−7.2	$615,363	3.3	$ 992,750
$ 71,261	1978	6.6	$580,012	2.1	$ 940,840
$ 73,755	1979	18.4	$599,408	6	$ 919,110
$ 76,337	1980	32.4	$692,547	6.4	$ 896,711
$ 79,009	1981	−4.9	$583,475	10.5	$ 903,561
$ 81,774	1982	21.4	$609,065	26.1	$1,036,273
$ 84,636	1983	22.5	$642,425	8.6	$1,033,478
$ 87,598	1984	6.3	$589,781	14.4	$1,082,087
$ 90,664	1985	32.2	$659,833	18.1	$1,170,870
$ 93,837	1986	18.5	$670,705	13.1	$1,218,124
$ 97,122	1987	5.2	$603,409	3.7	$1,162,479
$100,521	1988	16.8	$587,374	6.7	$1,133,110
$104,039	1989	31.5	$635,585	12.7	$1,159,762
$107,681	1990	−3.2	$511,011	9.2	$1,148,873
$111,449	1991	30.5	$521,429	14.6	$1,188,888
$115,350	1992	7.7	$437,347	7.2	$1,150,833
$119,387	1993	10	$349,755	8.8	$1,122,212
$123,566	1994	1.3	$229,130	−2.2	$ 976,676
$127,891	1995	37.4	$139,102	15.3	$ 978,650
$132,367	1996	23.1	$ 8,291	4.1	$ 880,981

Source: Dimensional Fund Advisors

numbers that we saw in Figure 9.2—compared with the 60/40 mix of Your Perfect Portfolio.

By the end of 2004, Your Perfect Portfolio had grown to nearly $13.8 million—enough to fund many more years of the scheduled withdrawals while leaving plenty of extra for lifetime gifts and generous bequests.

Table 13.4

Retiring on $1 Million: 50/50 and Your Perfect Portfolio Compared

Withdrawal	Year	50% global equity	Your Perfect Portfolio
$ 60,000	1970	$ 983,482	$ 969,742
$ 62,100	1971	$1,092,014	$ 1,098,012
$ 64,274	1972	$1,177,942	$ 1,211,411
$ 66,523	1973	$1,030,350	$ 1,033,362
$ 68,851	1974	$ 872,609	$ 843,978
$ 71,261	1975	$1,022,048	$ 1,019,159
$ 73,755	1976	$1,117,778	$ 1,128,316
$ 76,337	1977	$1,179,789	$ 1,216,327
$ 79,009	1978	$1,294,997	$ 1,368,932
$ 81,774	1979	$1,363,749	$ 1,452,967
$ 84,636	1980	$1,517,034	$ 1,645,630
$ 87,598	1981	$1,598,697	$ 1,719,159
$ 90,664	1982	$1,790,424	$ 1,914,533
$ 93,837	1983	$2,026,347	$ 2,221,368
$ 97,122	1984	$2,087,014	$ 2,287,961
$100,521	1985	$2,588,614	$ 2,908,911
$104,039	1986	$3,082,079	$ 3,537,957
$107,681	1987	$3,328,269	$ 3,885,212
$111,449	1988	$3,732,599	$ 4,461,008
$115,350	1989	$4,216,069	$ 5,135,715
$119,387	1990	$3,983,826	$ 4,760,036
$123,566	1991	$4,634,938	$ 5,648,702
$127,891	1992	$4,721,773	$ 5,772,500
$132,367	1993	$5,430,691	$ 6,796,925
$137,000	1994	$5,312,796	$ 6,718,696
$141,795	1995	$5,969,078	$ 7,643,093
$146,758	1996	$6,452,126	$ 8,340,648
$151,894	1997	$6,710,529	$ 8,717,224
$157,210	1998	$7,039,942	$ 9,190,703
$162,713	1999	$7,801,219	$10,421,765
$168,408	2000	$7,713,467	$10,256,564
$174,302	2001	$7,703,284	$10,224,119
$180,402	2002	$7,424,935	$ 9,736,760
$186,717	2003	$8,966,942	$12,289,118
$193,252	2004	$9,816,841	$13,797,592
	Total withdrawals	$4,000,441	$4,000,441

Now I'd like you to consider Table 13.5 which shows two distribution plans using Your Perfect Portfolio with real returns from 1970 through 2004. On the left is the portfolio we just saw. On the right is a more aggressive withdrawal plan that did not hold up past 2001. I think the message is unmistakable: for retirees who don't want to outlive their money, less (a lower withdrawal rate) is more. This is one of the most important topics retirees must come to grips with.

The fixed withdrawal plans we've been looking at, in which your retirement income is known in advance, may seem to give a comforting amount of security to retirees. But they are traps. The scheduled withdrawals in the aggressive plan in Table 13.5 put too big a strain on this portfolio. The conservative retiree in this scenario is likely at some point to want to spend more money than this schedule dictates. (In 1989, to pick an example at random, a $115,350 withdrawal from a portfolio worth $4.4 million would probably seem quite parsimonious.)

Retirees, whether they're on relatively tight budgets or have more money than they know what to do with, need to find the right balance between security and the freedom to "live it up" by spending money they can afford to spend. Most people will find that balance in a variable withdrawal schedule based on their actual portfolio performance each year.

When we started the fixed schedules at $60,000 and $80,000, those figures weren't derived from retirees' annual needs. They were calculated as the percentages of a $1 million portfolio. If the portfolio were larger, the beginning withdrawals would be larger, and vice versa.

In the variable withdrawal plan, that same calculation is made every year by applying a fixed percentage (6 percent or 8 percent in our examples) to the actual value of the portfolio at the end of each year. This approach has the great advantage of imposing some automatic feedback, decreasing retirees' spending when their portfolios are struggling and increasing spending when their investments are doing well. This discipline can force retirees with limited resources to keep their spending in check

Table 13.5

Retiring on $1 Million with Your Perfect Portfolio: Conservative ($60,000) versus Aggressive ($80,000) Withdrawals

	Conservative schedule			Aggressive schedule	
Withdrawal	End-of-year balance	Year	Withdrawal	End-of-year balance	
$ 60,000	$ 969,742	1970	$ 80,000	$ 949,109
$ 62,100	$ 1,098,012	1971	$ 82,800	$1,047,687
$ 64,274	$ 1,211,411	1972	$ 85,698	$1,126,784
$ 66,523	$ 1,033,362	1973	$ 88,697	$ 936,415
$ 68,851	$ 843,978	1974	$ 91,802	$ 738,509
$ 71,261	$ 1,019,159	1975	$ 95,015	$ 847,805
$ 73,755	$ 1,128,316	1976	$ 98,340	$ 893,384
$ 76,337	$ 1,216,327	1977	$101,782	$ 913,809
$ 79,009	$ 1,368,932	1978	$105,345	$ 971,221
$ 81,774	$ 1,452,967	1979	$109,032	$ 971,043
$ 84,636	$ 1,645,630	1980	$112,848	$1,029,448
$ 87,598	$ 1,719,159	1981	$116,798	$1,004,232
$ 90,664	$ 1,914,533	1982	$120,885	$1,035,207
$ 93,837	$ 2,221,368	1983	$125,116	$1,106,634
$ 97,122	$ 2,287,961	1984	$129,496	$1,048,886
$100,521	$ 2,908,911	1985	$134,028	$1,211,863
$104,039	$ 3,537,957	1986	$138,719	$1,348,852
$107,681	$ 3,885,212	1987	$143,574	$1,360,623
$111,449	$ 4,461,008	1988	$148,599	$1,427,822
$115,350	$ 5,135,715	1989	$153,800	$1,500,510
$119,387	$ 4,760,036	1990	$159,183	$1,268,518
$123,566	$ 5,648,702	1991	$164,755	$1,339,013
$127,891	$ 5,772,500	1992	$170,521	$1,216,671
$132,367	$ 6,796,925	1993	$176,489	$1,247,442
$137,000	$ 6,718,696	1994	$182,666	$1,068,918
$141,795	$ 7,643,093	1995	$189,060	$1,016,240
$146,758	$ 8,340,648	1996	$195,677	$ 906,815
$151,894	$ 8,717,224	1997	$202,525	$ 743,919
$157,210	$ 9,190,703	1998	$209,614	$ 568,090
$162,713	$10,421,765	1999	$216,950	$ 399,751
$168,408	$10,256,564	2000	$224,543	$ 171,251
$174,302	$10,224,119	2001	$232,403	**Broke!**
$180,402	$ 9,736,760	2002	$240,537	
$186,717	$12,289,118	2003	$248,955	
$193,252	$13,797,592	2004	$257,669	

while encouraging those with plenty of money to use their resources to enhance their own lives or their children's lives.

Again using real-life returns from 1970 through 2004, we show two variable withdrawal plans for Your Perfect Portfolio in Table 13.6. The conservative plan withdraws 6 percent of the portfolio value each year; the aggressive plan takes out 8 percent.

The comparison is interesting. It shows that for retirees who live long enough, less (conservative withdrawals in the beginning) becomes more (larger withdrawals in later years). If you study the numbers you'll find that after 13 years, in 1983, the conservative withdrawals become larger than the aggressive ones. The difference increases every year.

The conservative plan is better suited for early retirees, who might be able to supplement their withdrawals with part-time work for a few years and who would likely be around to reap the rewards of higher retirement withdrawals later. And of course it's better for people with limited resources. If they are fortunate enough to experience a string of robust portfolio years early in retirement, they'll gain more comfort (and more spending power) as time goes on. The aggressive plan is better suited to people who retire later—or those who have plenty of money beyond their needs.

Choosing between these two plans is also a choice between the relative importance of taking retirement income and leaving money in your estate. This is most dramatically illustrated in Table 13.5, in which one fixed-withdrawal plan leaves a portfolio worth $13.8 million and the other goes broke.

In my workshops, I've been asked many times about a "flexible-variable" plan that would withdraw a higher percentage immediately after good market years and revert to a more conservative percentage after poorer years.

Obviously there are many ways one could construct such a plan. You'll see one possibility in Table 13.7. On the left, for reference, is the conservative "variable" schedule from Table 13.6. On the right is what I consider a conservative "flexible-variable schedule.

Table 13.6

Retiring on $1 Million with Your Perfect Portfolio: Variable Withdrawals (6% versus 8%)

Conservative schedule			Aggressive schedule	
Withdrawal	End-of-year balance	Year	Withdrawal	End-of-year balance
$ 60,000	$ 969,742	1970	$ 80,000	$ 949,109
$ 58,185	$1,102,791	1971	$ 75,929	$1,056,074
$ 66,167	$1,214,806	1972	$ 84,486	$1,138,102
$ 72,888	$1,030,652	1973	$ 91,048	$ 944,545
$ 61,839	$ 847,782	1974	$ 75,564	$ 759,982
$ 50,867	$1,051,361	1975	$ 60,799	$ 921,816
$ 63,082	$1,179,841	1976	$ 73,745	$1,011,659
$ 70,790	$1,282,703	1977	$ 80,933	$1,075,327
$ 76,962	$1,451,725	1978	$ 86,026	$1,189,820
$ 87,103	$1,540,796	1979	$ 95,186	$1,234,601
$ 92,448	$1,742,256	1980	$ 98,768	$1,364,756
$104,535	$1,807,376	1981	$109,180	$1,384,088
$108,443	$1,997,592	1982	$110,727	$1,495,433
$119,855	$2,291,106	1983	$119,635	$1,676,706
$137,466	$2,319,595	1984	$134,136	$1,659,591
$139,176	$2,899,414	1985	$132,767	$2,027,896
$173,965	$3,437,332	1986	$162,232	$2,350,560
$206,240	$3,658,926	1987	$188,045	$2,446,572
$219,536	$4,064,782	1988	$195,726	$2,657,631
$243,887	$4,514,295	1989	$212,611	$2,886,132
$270,858	$4,025,380	1990	$230,891	$2,516,619
$241,523	$4,608,221	1991	$201,330	$2,816,841
$276,493	$4,527,443	1992	$225,347	$2,706,023
$271,647	$5,126,435	1993	$216,482	$2,995,812
$307,586	$4,859,234	1994	$239,665	$2,776,616
$291,554	$5,305,545	1995	$222,129	$2,964,041
$318,333	$5,546,159	1996	$237,123	$3,029,483
$332,770	$5,546,981	1997	$242,359	$2,962,463
$332,819	$5,595,278	1998	$236,997	$2,921,580
$335,717	$6,068,081	1999	$233,726	$3,097,636
$364,085	$5,702,546	2000	$247,811	$2,846,077
$342,153	$5,432,447	2001	$227,686	$2,650,471
$325,947	$4,947,127	2002	$212,038	$2,359,301
$296,828	$5,979,612	2003	$188,744	$2,786,943
$358,777	$6,407,331	2004	$222,955	$2,919,043

The flexible-variable plan works like this: After a year with portfolio returns under 12 percent (which I expect will be roughly half the time with Your Perfect Portfolio), the withdrawal is 6 percent of the ending portfolio value. After a year with returns of 12 percent or more, the distribution is 8 percent.

You'll see that this flexible-variable schedule started with a $60,000 withdrawal in 1970, because 1969 was a very disappointing year. (That year, U.S. small-cap stocks fell 26 percent, the S&P 500 Index was down 8.5 percent, and long-term corporate bonds had a negative total return of 8.1 percent.) You'll also immediately see that the flexible-variable plan resulted in some huge, abrupt decreases in income. A retiree who took out $95,100 in 1973 had to make do with only $48,692 two years later. This obviously isn't a suitable plan for somebody who must have a minimum $60,000, with some inflation protection, every year.

The flexible-variable plan produced higher withdrawals in 13 of the first 19 years in this table, but not once after that. However, you shouldn't read too much into the flexible-variable results shown in this table. If the same annual returns had come in a different order, the results could have been much different.

There are other "rules" that could be added to such a plan. For example you could specify that the withdrawal would always be at least the starting value, in this case $60,000, in order to assure you of at least a basic income. If your portfolio suffered a series of bad years, this would require you to absorb the effects of inflation while waiting for a recovery. But you wouldn't have to give up your basic needs.

The danger here is that one rule gets piled on top of another until the plan is a complex series of reactions to whatever unwanted thing just happened. I don't think retirees should be encouraged to keep fiddling with a withdrawal system in hopes of extracting short-term advantages. Choosing your withdrawal method is a complicated and critical step. Do it very carefully, if necessary with the help of a good adviser, and then stick to your plan. If you take a moderate approach that's based on conserva-

Table 13.7

Retiring on $1 Million with Your Perfect Portfolio: Conservative Withdrawals, Variable versus Flexible-Variable"

Variable withdrawals			Flexible-variable withdrawals	
Withdrawal	End-of-year balance	Year	Withdrawal	End-of-year balance
$ 60,000	$ 969,742	1970	$ 60,000	$ 969,742
$ 58,185	$1,102,791	1971	$ 58,185	$1,102,791
$ 66,167	$1,214,806	1972	$ 88,223	$1,188,745
$ 72,888	$1,030,652	1973	$ 95,100	$ 986,804
$ 61,839	$ 847,782	1974	$ 59,208	$ 811,530
$ 50,867	$1,051,361	1975	$ 48,692	$1,006,223
$ 63,082	$1,179,841	1976	$ 80,498	$1,104,662
$ 70,790	$1,282,703	1977	$ 88,373	$1,174,792
$ 76,962	$1,451,725	1978	$ 93,983	$1,300,512
$ 87,103	$1,540,796	1979	$104,041	$1,350,060
$ 92,448	$1,742,256	1980	$108,005	$1,493,030
$104,535	$1,807,376	1981	$119,442	$1,514,772
$108,443	$1,997,592	1982	$ 90,886	$1,673,105
$119,855	$2,291,106	1983	$133,848	$1,876,742
$137,466	$2,319,595	1984	$150,139	$1,858,319
$139,176	$2,899,414	1985	$111,499	$2,321,326
$173,965	$3,437,332	1986	$185,706	$2,691,719
$206,240	$3,658,926	1987	$215,338	$2,802,605
$219,536	$4,064,782	1988	$224,208	$3,045,359
$243,887	$4,514,295	1989	$243,629	$3,308,179
$270,858	$4,025,380	1990	$264,654	$2,885,423
$241,523	$4,608,221	1991	$173,125	$3,301,241
$276,493	$4,527,443	1992	$264,099	$3,172,392
$271,647	$5,126,435	1993	$190,344	$3,590,051
$307,586	$4,859,234	1994	$287,204	$3,328,517
$291,554	$5,305,545	1995	$199,711	$3,632,148
$318,333	$5,546,159	1996	$290,572	$3,713,770
$332,770	$5,546,981	1997	$222,826	$3,712,316
$332,819	$5,595,278	1998	$222,739	$3,742,615
$335,717	$6,068,081	1999	$224,557	$4,056,689
$364,085	$5,702,546	2000	$324,535	$3,729,009
$342,153	$5,432,447	2001	$223,741	$3,550,386
$325,947	$4,947,127	2002	$213,023	$3,231,291
$296,828	$5,979,612	2003	$193,877	$3,903,130
$358,777	$6,407,331	2004	$312,250	$4,090,740

tive assumptions, you'll stack the odds in your favor for having enough money to live it up in retirement and leave a satisfying legacy behind.

Beyond the Formulas

Real-life situations almost always require more than formulas you can find in a book. The emotional and psychological hurdles can be more formidable than the strictly financial ones. Some retirees are very disturbed if they must "invade" their principal, even though the invasion might be only a minor scratch.

I recall a couple of clients, Mel and Christie, who retired with $1.2 million, which we invested in a combination of equity and fixed-income funds with risk and return characteristics that were suited to their needs. From this portfolio, they needed only $36,000 a year.

Mel and Christie were upset one year after we sold a little bit of their equity holdings in order to raise the $36,000. To them, that was simply unacceptable.

Our solution was to put enough of the account into fixed-income funds—in this case it turned out to be $750,000—to generate the needed income entirely from interest and dividends. The rest remained in equity funds, which went untouched. This wasn't necessarily the most efficient use of this couple's money. But it made them comfortable enough to stick with the plan.

For clients who want psychological insulation between themselves and the market, we sometimes use a three-pronged approach. Each year we start with one full year of the client's desired income in a money market fund, where it can't suffer any losses. The client draws on this money through the year, gradually reducing the balance.

We put a second year's income into a short-term bond fund, where it is relatively stable. The rest of the portfolio goes into whatever mix of equities and fixed-income funds is appropriate for the client.

In theory, at the end of each year we replenish the money market fund from the bond fund, which in turn is replenished from the long-term portfolio. In practice, we don't touch the short-term bond part of the portfolio; instead we move money directly from the long-term investments to the money market fund. This makes the client more comfortable and bolsters the fixed-income part of the overall portfolio.

There are other emotional challenges. One of our clients, an engineer named Henry with a frugal lifestyle and strong savings habits, started with a retirement fund of more than $4 million and a home he owned free and clear. His annual cost of living was $60,000—a relatively tiny burden for his portfolio. A few years after Henry retired, his wife, Linda, was diagnosed with cancer. Although she could function quite well, Linda feared that her remaining lifetime was limited and expressed a strong desire to travel. Henry, knowing that travel can be expensive, balked.

Henry was very frightened about running out of money, and his fear was grounded in his past. When he was a child, he and his family experienced the trauma of living through World War II in Germany. After the war, for a time they lived in a garage in South America. Later he arrived in the United States without a penny to his name.

The problem was psychological, not financial. We helped him use affirmations about the role that money could and should play in his life. After a while he saw that hoarding his assets would not do him or Linda any good. Henry realized he could easily afford to use some of those assets to be supportive of his wife—which he did. Years later, Linda is still in remission and they are both happier than if they had continued to be miserly.

Some retirees figure out their own creative solutions. I recall a successful businessman named Art, who had grown up in poverty. Even though he eventually became president of a small bank in California, Art always thought of himself as a very poor person. I knew him as a legendary tightwad. One day I ran into Art at a conference. He told me he and his wife had just returned from a very expensive round-the-world trip. Frankly I was shocked to hear this, even though I knew they had plenty of money. I was even more surprised when Art told me their children had paid for the trip. "We started to spend our children's inheritance," he reported with a grin.

When Art and his wife, June, regarded their money as belonging to them (which of course it did), it was too painful to part with it. But when they started thinking of it as belonging to their children, all of whom were doing fine financially on their own, Art and June could loosen up and start spending. (The children, Art told me, were all in favor of the idea.)

Chapter FOURTEEN

Hiring an Investment Adviser

I found the best way to give advice to my children is to find out what they want and then advise them to do it.

—Harry Truman

A few years ago during the tough days of the 2000–2002 bear market, Oppenheimer Funds Inc. did a nationwide survey of several hundred investors with investment assets of at least $25,000. Half the subjects had financial advisers and half reported that they made their own decisions. The responses to one question in particular stood out to me:

Question: Do you believe it's important to have a diversified portfolio? Answers: Of investors with advisers, 94 percent said yes versus 22 percent for do-it-yourself investors. This survey wasn't scientific, and Oppenheimer of course had an axe to grind. Nevertheless, those answers tell me that advisers apparently are teaching clients about the value of diversification.

One other response indicated that investors with advisers were nearly three times as likely to expect a comfortable retirement as those without advisers. Just what that means is open to interpretation. But there is clearly some correlation between having advisers and feeling confident about the future.

Investing is a complex business with many facets that must be successfully managed in order to assure a successful outcome. I may be biased in my view, but nearly 40 years of being involved with Wall Street has shown me over and over that it's too much for most individuals to do on their own. I believe you'll greatly increase your probability of success if you have an adviser. Finding the right adviser is critical, however. There's bad news and good news.

The bad news is that every year millions of investors get poor advice, and some of them get fleeced, from brokers who don't have the training, the experience, the knowledge, or the incentives to give investors the help they need. Worse, most of those brokers have conflicts of interest with their clients.

The good news is that the fastest-growing segment of the financial services industry is made up of independent advisers. Investors who are willing to do their homework and who know what to look for can find excellent advisers whose interests match those of their clients.

To avoid conflicts of interest, you must understand compensation. At the heart of compensation is a question: Who's paying the adviser? Advisers work for whoever pays them. Whoever "writes the check" is the employer to whom the adviser owes his or her loyalty.

The topic of compensation can seem complicated, but in fact it boils down to one of two equations. To put it bluntly, an adviser whose compensation comes from an insurance company, a mutual fund company, a brokerage house, or any other financial services company is not working for you. In this equation, the adviser is using you as a tool to fulfill the objectives of some company. An adviser whose compensation comes exclusively from clients, on the other hand, is working for those clients. In this equation, the adviser is using financial products as the tools to fulfill your objectives.

You can choose whichever one of these equations seems better to you. Your choice will determine the quality of advice you get.

To maximize the probability of finding the right adviser, seek one who is independent and whose interests are aligned with yours. If you find the right adviser and use him or her well, you are likely to get several results:

- You are likely to make more money.
- You are likely to make more money at less risk.
- You are likely to have less anxiety about your investments.
- You are more likely to maintain the discipline necessary to be successful.
- You are more likely to reach your financial goals.
- You will free your time and your mind for other priorities in life.

I f I did a perfect job writing this book, you wouldn't need to hire a professional adviser. You would know exactly what to do and how to manage your emotions and your risks. At most, you'd need a coach and a cheerleader. But that's a fantasy, and fantasy can be deadly for investors. Investing may seem simple: Buy low, sell high. What else do you need to know? To name a few, tax implications, asset allocation, and risk analysis are all essential. Yet it is rare that I encounter an investor who understands these things and can properly apply them.

If you want to do better than most people, you have two choices: You can either acquire this knowledge or you can hire it. I'm convinced that you will have a much higher probability of success if you do the latter. Sometime in your life, you have undoubtedly hired someone to do something for you. Maybe the stakes were high, maybe not. If you hire the wrong person to cut your hair or the wrong person to paint your house, you may be embarrassed and frustrated. But the damage does not last forever, and you can recover. Good parents aren't casual about choosing somebody to care for young children. They know the stakes are high. Investors should adopt that same attitude when they choose somebody they will rely on for financial advice and money management skills.

Personally, I enjoy hiring people who are pleasant and nice and who make me feel good when I'm around them. But I know that if I want to get an important job done and the results are very important, "nice" just isn't enough. I want to hire the very best person—and you should, too.

So how do you find the best adviser? For starters, don't do what most casual investors do. Don't trust your finances to a broker. Every year investors lose millions of dollars at the hands of people they trust (but shouldn't) to give them financial advice. (For a look at why that happens, see the box on page 200.)

Instead, start by learning how to recognize and avoid conflicts of interest. To do this, you will have to ask questions that you might not want to ask, because they involve how your adviser is paid. Wall Street hopes you won't be too interested in the topic of compensation. But I hope you will be.

Your adviser is in business to make money; he or she will have thought long and hard about this topic. Any adviser worthy of your business will be happy to discuss compensation with you candidly and openly. If you encounter someone who wants to dodge the topic or gives you vague answers, look elsewhere.

Compensation for financial advice and services comes in four basic forms.

- First, your adviser can be paid on commissions generated when you make transactions. A stockbroker most likely earns a commission when you buy or sell a financial product. An adviser or salesperson gets a commission when you buy a load fund. For an early warning sign of a commission arrangement, look for the name of a big financial services company on the door of an adviser's office.

- Second, in a fee-only arrangement, you may pay the adviser by the hour, or perhaps a flat fee for specified services. You'll be buying only the adviser's time and expertise.

- Third, in a different fee-only arrangement, your adviser may be paid a small percentage of your assets periodically. This compensation grows or shrinks along with your assets. If your wealth grows, so does your adviser's pay.

- Fourth, there are incentive compensation programs that are legal only for accredited investors, somebody with a net worth of $1.5 million or more. An example of such an arrangement is for the adviser to receive a straight percentage of any investment gains, perhaps 10 or 20 percent. This sort of arrangement is common with hedge funds.

Each form of compensation gives the adviser a particular kind of incentive. You need to know what those incentives are.

When compensation is based on straight commissions, the adviser's incentive is to generate transactions. The more trading you do, the more commissions you generate. Furthermore, the broker or adviser who's paid on commissions has an incentive to encourage you to buy products that pay higher commissions.

Everybody in the financial industry (except, unfortunately, most of the clients) understands that the highest commissions are paid on the products that are hardest to sell. And what products are hardest to sell? Generally those that are most complex and most risky. Result: Many advisers are most enthusiastic about products that investors want and need the least.

When compensation involves only fees regardless of where you invest your money, the adviser has no financial incentive to steer you into certain products instead of others. The adviser is working just for you, and there's no conflict of interest.

When the adviser is paid based on assets under management, the adviser's incentive is to see your assets grow (and of course to persuade you to let him or her manage more of your assets). This aligns the adviser's interest with yours. This is the best way to pay somebody who takes responsibility for your finances.

Incentive programs seem like a great way to keep from paying when you are losing money or earning only a minimal return. Some of our clients with larger accounts like an arrangement in which we don't make a dime in a year unless they achieve at least some minimum return, typically 8 percent. They see this as a way to make sure we are on their side.

Of course we can't guarantee an 8 percent rate of return, and we therefore run the risk that we could have a year, or even a series of years, in which we get no compensation for managing the account. To compensate us for that risk, our agreement typically provides for a higher fee when the client does achieve the minimum target return. In some cases we charge 2 percent of the year-end account balance, roughly twice our normal fee.

One potential problem with an incentive fee arrangement is that your adviser might encourage you to take higher risks than you should. So make sure you are always investing within your risk tolerance. A good adviser wants you to be successful over a prolonged period, not generate a spectacular short-term return and then immediately crash and burn.

How do you bring up the subject of compensation when

you're interviewing a potential adviser? A great place to start is to simply ask if there will be any actual or potential conflicts of interest. Any good adviser should be pleased that you are savvy enough to ask such a question. If an adviser seems insulted by this question, this is not the right adviser for you.

Here's another good question that you should get in the habit of asking whenever an adviser makes a recommendation: "Why are you recommending this product to me?" Even better, ask for a written answer that addresses the potential return and potential risk and the cost (there is always a cost) to you of this particular investment. This single request, if it were regularly made by clients, would avoid billions of dollars worth of grief at the hands of advisers who are mostly just looking out for themselves and their sales goals.

When you're shopping for a financial adviser, here are the most important things to look for:

- Experience. Thorough training isn't enough. Your adviser should be somebody who's been in the trenches through good times and bad—and who has a successful track record through it all.

- Lots of knowledge about expenses, taxes, diversification, asset allocation, withdrawals, and risk management.

- A commitment to avoid conflicts of interest with you.

- A commitment to be available whenever you need something. One of my company's advisers makes a point to tell his clients to call him anytime, 24/7. If it's the middle of the night, they'll get his voice mail—which is the first thing he checks when he arrives at the office every morning.

- Someone who will listen to you and take you seriously when you aren't happy—even if you don't have more business to send his or her way.

At the end of my investing workshops I introduce my company's financial advisers, who I think are among the best in the business. I also offer, for anyone who would rather not do business with my company, to find an excellent independent adviser. For workshop participants who live in the Seattle area, I personally know a few advisers who I can recommend without any reservation.

For people who live elsewhere, here's how I would go about finding the right adviser: My first requirement would be somebody who's independent, without any relationship to a sales manager. My second requirement would be somebody who is compensated only by clients. I'm most likely to find these attributes, along with experience, knowledge, training and ethics, from a Certified Public Accountant who holds the Personal Finance Specialist (PFS) designation. (I know that any CPA will have a very healthy respect for expenses and taxes.) However, steer clear of CPAs who have aligned themselves with broker-dealers.

I would also look for somebody who has access to Dimensional Fund Advisors' asset class index funds, which I regard as the best mutual funds in the world (see Chapter 12).

If you can identify and interview three or four people who meet those criteria, you'll almost certainly find an excellent adviser. Whatever you pay such a person will most likely be one of the best investments you'll make.

Hiring a Broker: Why You Should Take a Pass

One of the biggest risks facing investors is what I call adviser risk, the possibility that you may lose money because of inappropriate professional advice.

Here's a simple recipe that's guaranteed to produce inappropriate advice: Start with a salesperson who's perceived as (and who is presenting himself or herself as) an adviser. Then add inexperience and ignorance. Top it off with a high-pressure conflict of interest.

Brokers may be friendly and pleasant to deal with. But they are not really your friends. A real friend doesn't exploit your lack of knowledge and sophistication.

Most investors need advisers. But brokers are not advisers, any more than people who sell cars are transportation consultants. Brokers keep their jobs based entirely on how well they meet sales targets and bring in revenue. If their clients do well or do poorly, that is essentially irrelevant from the perspective of the people who manage and motivate and evaluate brokers.

Brokers are not analysts. They are good at passing the tests required for licensing. They are good at sales. They are usually personable, outgoing, persistent, and easy to like. But most of them can't analyze securities or speak authoritatively about economics.

Ideally, an adviser's job is to solve problems (or take advantage of opportunities) for clients. That is not what brokers are trained, motivated, or paid to do. A broker's real job is to sell products. A good adviser should make sure clients understand the risks of investments before they are made. Brokers know that sales are generated by optimism and hope, not by worry and caution. Investors themselves are partly to blame for this. When all the customer seems to want is performance, and when the broker is under pressure to push certain products, why should a broker go out of his or her way to point out that these products will probably produce less performance than the investors want?

In my mind there is no question which choices investors would make if they knew all the facts. Almost without exception investors would choose funds with minimal fees, commissions, and expenses. But the typical broker never presents that material to the client. Instead, the broker goes right into an enthusiastic sales pitch for the products that are likely to be easy to sell.

Most clients have no idea of the pressures their brokers are under to sell. One broker told me in an e-mail: "There are a lot of good, well-meaning brokers at large retail brokerage firms who would like to recommend investments such as the ones you recommend. But they find themselves nearly coerced into recommending the higher commission products by the management of these firms."

What's always easy to sell is recent hot performance, not broad diversification into asset classes that may have been underperforming. Rare indeed is the broker who goes to the trouble of persuading clients to have a broad mix of large companies and small companies, growth companies and value companies, U.S. and international companies. In fact, I don't know that I've ever seen a brokerage client whose portfolio is as widely diversified as it should be.

For more on why I think you should avoid brokers, visit the web site for this book and read an article called "Why Your Broker Might Not Really Be Your Friend." This is not personal. I have many friends who are brokers, and I enjoy them and respect them. However, I believe investors deserve the best investment and planning advice available. They are highly unlikely to get it from somebody whose job is to sell them commissioned products.

I know that many brokers try hard to do their best to do the right thing for clients. But most clients have no way to know which brokers those are. I have been in this business for decades and have lots of good contacts, and even I still do not know any reliable way to identify brokers who are truly worth trusting. Although they are in the financial services industry, I don't believe brokers are in the same business as I am. And I have stopped recommending that people go to brokers at all.

What You Should Get From an Investment Adviser

Professional investment advice goes far beyond recommendations for putting together a portfolio. A good adviser should be able to help you:

- Define your financial needs and turn them into specific, measurable objectives.

- Project your income and savings.

- Project your investment returns.

- Project your future portfolio values.

- Project your cash flow in retirement.

- Determine the most desirable mix of investments to achieve your individual needs.

- Complete paperwork.

- Open custodial accounts if you need or want them.

- Manage investments and regularly review your objectives.

- Research investments to improve your results.

- Manage your money on a full-time basis if that is what you desire.

- Get objective guidance on all financial matters.

Other valuable services an adviser may offer include advice on assets the adviser is not managing, advice to other members of your family, negotiating loans you may make to your children or other family members, and making referrals to other professionals whose services you may need. In addition, a good adviser can help resolve differences between couples.

An adviser who does all these things well is likely to be among your most important assets.

Chapter FIFTEEN

Your Action Plan

■■■■■

*The person who does things makes many mistakes.
But he never makes the biggest mistake of all: doing
nothing.*

—Benjamin Franklin

By this point I hope you understand that the most important decision investors must make is their choice of assets. The asset allocation you choose will have more impact on your long-term returns than your timing of sales and purchases. In the long run, your asset allocation will have more impact than your selection of mutual funds.

But neither your timing nor your investment selection is the second most important decision. Your No. 2 decision is every bit as important as asset allocation—and for some investors it's the toughest decision of all: the decision to make a change. Nothing I write can make you change. I'm an educator and an adviser, not a salesman. It's my job to inform you and convince you and persuade you, but not to manipulate you into doing something, even if I believe it's in your best interests.

Sometimes change is hard because the task looks overwhelming. In this chapter I've made a list, trying to break down many of the essential steps you should take into small enough tasks that you can tackle them. My purpose is to help you when you get "stuck" because of inertia or any other reason. The list that follows isn't comprehensive. But if you ever are unsure what to do next, this chapter should give you plenty of tasks to do (or review if you've already done them).

At the end you will find what I think of as the ultimate (not a word I use lightly, but it applies here) way to get yourself unstuck, no matter what.

I'd like to start with a true story.

In the autumn of 2001, a time that turned out to be about midway through the great bear market at the start of this century, a prospective client came into our office and asked an unusual question: Why hadn't he done what he knew he should do with his investment portfolio?

This man was sophisticated and well informed about financial matters, a professional in his fifties who had managed to accumulate more than $1 million for his retirement. We had met with this investor almost a year earlier and tried to get him to diversify his portfolio, most of which was invested in technology stocks and technology funds. He had attended two workshops that I led and had heard me speak on another occasion. Without any doubt, he knew he needed to make some major changes in his portfolio.

When he returned to our office that fall, he had lost more than 60 percent of the value of his portfolio since the bull market peaked a year and a half earlier, in early 2000. The losses had set him back years in his goal of retiring early. Even as we talked, the market continued to deteriorate.

"Why haven't I done what I know I should do?" he asked. "Why didn't you tell me something that would have motivated me to make this obvious change?" This intelligent, accomplished man was staring into the face of whether or not to take action. In every area of life, there's a big difference between knowing that you should do something and actually doing it.

He was essentially telling me that I had convinced him that he should have a more diversified portfolio, but that I had not persuaded him to do anything about it. He was right, of course. And he was not alone.

At a workshop two weeks later, I asked for a show of hands. "How many of you have made major changes in your investments in the past year and a half?" About 5 percent of the hands went up. "How many of you wish you had made major changes in your investments?" A majority of hands were raised.

Few of us are immune from the "diseases" of habit and inertia. I smoked cigarettes for several years when I was young, even though I knew it was bad for my health. I've struggled for many years with keeping my weight and my diet under control and maintaining an exercise program that I know would be good for me.

I can't push you over whatever psychological hump may keep you from doing what you need to do. But I can offer you a laundry list of individual steps you can take to get from wherever you are to wherever you wish or need to be. Therefore, without further ado, here are some of the most important tasks that will get your financial affairs in order and clear the decks for that perfect retirement you want.

■ Make a balance sheet that lists all your assets and liabilities.

■ Review your investments to make sure your overall asset allocation includes all parts of your portfolio.

■ Use the Instant X-Ray portfolio analysis tool at Morningstar.com to analyze your investments. Use this to determine your stock overlap, your asset class distribution, and your overall expense level.

■ Break down your portfolio by what's in taxable accounts and what's in tax-sheltered ones. Determine the extent to which you have your most tax-efficient holdings in taxable accounts (where they belong) and your least tax-efficient holdings in tax shelters (where they belong).

■ Make a written retirement plan, using a notebook or a folder in your computer. Use this to collect portfolio values, questions and topics to discuss with your adviser, an overall description of your estate plan, income and expense projections, and any other investment-related and retirement-related materials you may want at hand. Include a "front page" document that notes your desired retirement date and the size of portfolio you'll need at that time to meet both your basic target and your live it up target.

■ Analyze your spending to make sure it is under control.

■ Hire an adviser, if you don't already have one, using the guidelines you'll find in Chapter 14.

■ Meet with your spouse or partner, if you have one, to discuss your goals and your worries about retirement.

■ Educate yourself beyond what's in this book, using recommendations in the Appendix and the online links you'll find on the web site for the book.

■ Once every year, reread Chapter 4 to remind yourself of your three biggest adversaries: Wall Street, the media, and your own emotions.

- If you have a spouse or partner, discuss your estate plan with him or her.

- If your will doesn't do what you want, meet with your attorney to write a new one. If you don't have a will and an estate plan, make this your top priority.

- Meet with your adviser to write an investment policy statement.

- Sell any investments you own that are in the wrong asset classes for your needs.

- Sell any investments you own that have excessive continuing expenses.

- Sell any investments you own that will saddle you with excessive taxes.

- If you are investing regularly or want to invest regularly, establish automatic investment plans with your mutual funds or arrange for payroll deductions.

- Schedule one day a year when you will rebalance your portfolio to meet your target allocations.

- If you are in or near retirement, review your withdrawal plan with your financial adviser.

- If you find yourself watching CNBC more than one hour a month, use your cable box to block that channel so it can't get to your television.

Finally, as promised: If you're feeling stuck and all else fails, pick up the phone and schedule a consultation with your adviser. If you have picked the right adviser, one who isn't motivated to sell you products, that adviser can quickly figure out what—if anything—would be the best use of your time and energy at any given moment in your life.

If you take this to heart, you'll never end up in my office asking why I didn't "make" you do the right thing. More likely, you'll be living it up in retirement. And that's exactly what I want!

Merriman on Doing It Now

Many times investors go to the trouble of figuring out what they should do, only to be stopped by the thought that they should wait for the right time.

A typical comment I hear goes like this: "OK, Paul, I can see what I should do to properly diversify my portfolio. But because of what's happening in the market these days I think I should wait a bit."

The reason for waiting is usually some variation on "until things settle down" or "until it's more obvious which way this market is going." Sometimes the reasons are legitimate, such as minimizing taxes or early-withdrawal penalties. But quite often, there's no compelling reason.

Still, it's common to find yourself in this situation: You have determined that what you are currently doing is not the right thing for you. And you have determined something else that *is* the right thing for you. And yet it seems like this is the wrong time to make the change.

When you find yourself in that spot, here's a formula that's worthwhile remembering:

It is never the wrong time to do the right thing. But it is always the wrong time to keep doing the wrong thing.

Henry Kissinger said it another way: "A problem ignored is a crisis invited."

Chapter SIXTEEN

My 500-Year Plan

■■■■■

Diamonds are only lumps of coal that stuck to their jobs for a long time.

—B.C. Forbes

If you are fortunate enough to have surplus funds left when you complete your life, there is an enormous opportunity to do some things with this leftover money. It's called estate planning.

Attitudes are gradually evolving about the ways people leave money to their heirs, and my own views have changed over the years. I have decided that when I finally must leave this life, I don't want my estate to simply write big checks to my children and grandchildren. I want the financial results of my life's work to amount to more than lump-sum bequests.

Encouraged by the possibilities of Your Perfect Portfolio described in Part II of this book, coupled with the variable withdrawal schedules we saw in Chapter 13, I have devised a

500-year plan for my money. Unfortunately, I won't be around to see how it works. But here's the overall plan: I'm going to leave money in a way that will supplement my family's own income and perhaps will give them opportunities they wouldn't ever have otherwise. And my estate plan will ultimately provide continuing support to charitable causes which I believe are worthy of this money.

This plan is the result of a great deal of thought and discussion, and I know it's not what most people would want to do. But I'm sharing it with readers of this book in the hope it will stimulate their own thinking about the legacies they may want to leave.

In the 1960s, when I first began working with people on their finances, an important priority for many older people was the desire to eventually leave substantial bequests to their children. This was—and remains—a worthy goal. Economists generally believe that trillions of dollars will be left to the next generation over the next 30 years. This massive transfer of wealth will have profound effects, individually and collectively.

Some fundamental things have changed in the past 40 years. The take-it-for-granted confidence of the 1960s has been all but wiped out. Social Security has an unknown future. The high inflation of the 1970s and 1980s mangled many fortunes that were comfortably invested in bonds that most people thought were safe. Retirement pensions, once a staple of old-age expectations and once the responsibility of employers, have gradually been replaced by defined-contribution arrangements such as 401(k) plans and IRAs.

Individuals are now the ones who must make the decisions about their investments. And they are the ones who must accept the risks involved in those decisions. Gradually but irresistibly, corporations—and society—have become somewhat less paternalistic. Perhaps I have done the same. I like to think I have adopted a more enlightened paternalism. As much as I love and treasure my children and grandchildren, I do not want my success in life to relieve them of the responsibility to provide for themselves. In addition, I know that my wish to be generous extends far beyond my family.

My first priority is to see that my wife has adequate resources to live well for the rest of her life. My estate plan provides for that, and we have set aside other investments for our children. She and I have committed together to the rest of the following plan.

My goal for my estate is to leave something akin to a pension fund for each of my children and grandchildren that will provide a growing annual income to them. I want the assets to be protected from as many of the potential threats as possible that they could face after my death. If I left assets outright to my heirs, some or all of those assets could be lost to divorce, lawsuits, poor investment decisions, or creditors—not to mention an heir who might decide to squander the wealth I have carefully acquired by spending it on short-term high living, only to be left high and dry later. I don't want that.

I have concluded that the best protection against such contingencies is to use trusts. That way, the assets can be invested and still be kept out of reach of most, if not all, financial predators.

Here is my 500-year plan:

My estate will create a charitable remainder trust for each of my four children. The money is to be invested along the lines of Your Perfect Portfolio, with a 60/40 split of equities and fixed-income funds. This portfolio is likely to grow over time, while the fixed-income allocation and wide diversification of equity asset classes should protect against major losses.

Each year, the trustee will tally up the assets in each trust and pay 5 percent of the total to the beneficiary. As we saw in Chapter 13, this combination of diversified investments and modest withdrawals has a high likelihood of not only surviving but also of growing over time. And if the fund grows, so do the annual payments to my children. Assuming taxes and expenses can be kept to a minimum, that growth is likely to be greater than inflation, providing actual growth in real value.

My wife and I each have educational and charitable causes that we care deeply about. At times that we hope will be long in the future, at the end of the lifetime of each of our children, the assets in the trust for that child will go to the Seattle Foundation. The foundation will invest the money, most likely following a plan similar to the standard 60/40 pension model that we discussed in Chapter 6. Each year, the foundation will pay 5 percent of the money to charities we have designated.

I chose the Seattle Foundation for this because it gives me a convenient way to donate money to many legitimate tax-exempt organizations at a reasonable cost. Obviously, charitable causes that I choose today could, sometime in the next 500 years or so, outlive their usefulness or cease to exist. Under the terms of my bequest, the foundation will have the authority (and the duty) to substitute different organizations when appropriate. By using this foundation, I have in effect enlisted a team of people to make smart decisions and ensure that my assets will continue doing what I want them to do, regardless of future developments that I cannot possibly anticipate.

This is a permanent arrangement, and there is no ending time for it. Hence, my 500-year plan could theoretically last much longer than that. It's interesting to speculate on what such a bequest might be worth in 100 or 500 years. Doing so, of course, requires making some assumptions.

I have no idea how much my estate will leave to each of these trusts, but let's assume for example that I am able to leave $1 million for each of my children. (I hope the amount will be larger, but $1 million gives me a convenient way to crunch the numbers.) Assume further that after taxes, expenses, the annual payment, and inflation, the investments in each trust grow by 2.5 percent per year. I believe that's a conservative assumption, and there's a good chance the growth will be greater. But 2.5 percent is a rate that seems reasonably in the ballpark of what's probable.

By adjusting for inflation, I am able to think about the future results of this investment in constant dollars. I don't know now what $1 million will be worth when I die. But because I am adjusting all the numbers after my death for presumed inflation, these future amounts should be comparable to that $1 million.

Here's what that means: If the first annual payment to one of my children is $50,000, a later payment of $75,000 in these projections represents 50 percent more real wealth than the first payment. (If I didn't do this, the numbers over several hundred years would grow to be almost incomprehensible—and hard to believe.) Even with a low growth rate such as 2.5 percent, when you're dealing in hundreds of years, the numbers get pretty big!

In the first year after my death, each one of my surviving children would receive a payment of $50,000. I expect my two older children to outlive me by about 30 years. Twenty-five years after my death, presumably in one of the latter years of their lives, they would each receive $92,697. Since these are real (after inflation) dollars, by that time they will have received a significant "raise" from this pension-like trust.

The trusts for all four children will be created at the same time, soon after my death, and each year each of the four will receive equal payments. But two of my daughters will be younger when the payments start. I expect these two younger daughters to survive me by about 50 years. Forty years after my death, under these assumptions, these two daughters would each receive $134,253, and that payment would reach $171,855 by the 50th year after my death.

I think it's unlikely that any of my children will survive me by more than 60 years (though anything is possible, I suppose). At that time, my initial bequests of $4 million into four charitable remainder trusts would be worth about $17.6 million. By then it would be in the hands of the Seattle Foundation, which would make an annual payment to charities of $879,958 (the combined payout from the assets that had been in four trusts).

Project this out to 100 years after my death, and the charitable payment would be $2,362,753, a "dividend" of nearly 50 percent based on the $4 million left in my will. (Remember we are talking about constant dollars, so these numbers, relatively speaking, are "real.")

By 122 years after my death, the payout would grow to $4 million. In real terms, that would equal (every year) the entire amount that my estate put into the four trusts in the first place.

Predictably, the numbers keep growing. By 250 years after my death, the annual payout to charities is $96 million. By 500 years, my $4 million of bequests would pay out $25 billion a year—or 6,250 times the amount of wealth I left in these trusts. That's every year! The principal by then would be worth $500 billion. That's a big enough number that I'm content to stop the calculations right there.

Obviously this 500-year plan requires great patience, a commodity that should not pose any problem to me while I'm in the grave. However, it doesn't require extraordinary patience from my survivors, who will begin getting benefits right away.

This plan is my way to provide perpetual income to my heirs. I like to imagine that any heir who gets a check every year from Mom, Dad, Grandma, or Grandpa could easily develop warm, fuzzy feelings of appreciation. I know that sort of appreciation can stretch for generations and span centuries. One of my colleagues is among the owners of a sizeable piece of waterfront recreational property in the Seattle area that was purchased in 1905 by his great-grandfather. He and his many cousins use this place every summer, and they never tire of expressing their appreciation to their great-grandfather for making this available to the family.

My 500-year plan won't provide even close to everything that my children need, and it isn't designed to do that. It's designed to be "frosting on the cake." I hope it will let them do things that they might not otherwise be able to do.

Doing this is easier than you might think. The two most essential elements are good investments and a trust document. By now you should already know how to make good investments. You'll find a copy of the actual trust document on the web site for this book. The Seattle Foundation referred me to a local law firm that helped put together these charitable remainder trusts without any charge to me. (The law firm, which is retained by the foundation, didn't write my will but provided language for me to take to my own attorney.) I believe that many other community foundations have similar arrangements. One other benefit of this arrangement is that, because the money is destined ultimately to be donated to tax-exempt organizations, my estate will receive a tax credit at my death.

The 500-year plan is for my children. My grandchildren are beneficiaries of another arrangement that I described in an article (also available on the web site for this book) called "The Best Investment I Will Ever Make, or How to Turn $10,000 into $20 Million." This started in 1994 when my son, Jeff Merriman-Cohen, became a proud father (and I a proud grandfather). I wanted to do something really extraordinary for my new grandson, Aaron, and I spent a lot of time thinking about it.

I identified five things I wanted my gift to achieve. First, I wanted to make a one-time investment that would give Aaron a comfortable retirement. Second, the money was not to be used for anything before his 65th birthday. Third, there should be no tax liability on the growth and income of the investments. Fourth, at least $20 million should eventually go to charity. Finally, I wanted to do all this with a gift of only $10,000 up front.

With help from Jeff and some professional advisers, I found a way to accomplish all five objectives (although I paid legal fees of about $1,000 in addition to the $10,000 gift). Doing this required three things: time, a trust, and a variable annuity. It turned out that Aaron and I could accomplish this together as a grandpa/grandson team. He has the time but not the financial resources. I had the financial resources and the ability to make a plan, but not the time.

In a nutshell, here's how it worked: I made a one-time gift of $10,000 to an irrevocable trust for Aaron's benefit. His parents, Jeff and Barrie, are the trustees. The money is invested in a variable annuity, where it is compounding on a tax-deferred basis. Under the terms of the trust, Aaron cannot touch this money until he is 65. That leaves Jeff free to concentrate on long-term investments, which we expect to return 10 to 12 percent a year. Jeff, as trustee, chose to invest all the money in equities, half in U.S. funds, half in international funds.

If these investments can earn 11.3 percent annually, as similar asset combinations have done in the past, the trust portfolio will be worth $10 million in 2059, when Aaron is 65. Not bad for a $10,000 investment!

At that time, Aaron will receive annual payments of 7 percent of the trust's value, with the payments continuing for as long as he lives. That first payment could be for $700,000, which seems like a whopping amount until you remember that its purchasing power will be eroded by inflation. (Assuming inflation of 3 percent, that's the equivalent of about $131,000 in 2004 dollars. That's not enough to make Aaron wealthy, but certainly a very comfortable supplement to whatever he is able to accumulate on his own.)

If Aaron lives another 20 years and if the investments continue to earn 11.3 percent annually while paying out 7 percent every year, the trust should grow to be worth about $23 million by the time of Aaron's death. At the end of his lifetime, the assets in the trust will be given to tax-exempt organizations to be determined by the trustees, who could be Aaron's own children or grandchildren.

I have established similar trusts for my other grandchildren, and at this point everybody is happy about it.

When I put this plan together, a lot of friends and advisers told me I was making a big mistake. They said I was locking money away that Aaron might urgently need before he is 65. Some were incredulous that I would set up a plan under which Aaron, if he died at age 65½, would get only half a year of his "pension." Others criticized this plan for failing to provide for any family that Aaron may leave behind after his death.

Those are all valid criticisms, and the article on the web site for this book discusses my responses in detail. I'll hit a few highlights here.

I believe that anybody who won a lottery to be paid out at the rate of $700,000 a year for 20 years would consider himself or herself very fortunate. I have essentially given Aaron that winning lottery ticket, with two benefits that you won't find in any state lottery: The payments last as long as Aaron's life, and they will (presumably) grow over time.

This arrangement gives Aaron an incentive to take care of himself and live a long, healthy life. It lets him start thinking of himself as somebody who will one day have a lot of influence over how a very big chunk of money will be given to charitable causes. This also lets Aaron accumulate his own resources for an "early" retirement, should he choose it, with the "lotto" kicking in at age 65 to take care of him permanently after that.

The web site for this book contains the trust documents I used. You are welcome to take them to your attorney and modify them for your own situation.

I can't of course ever know the ultimate outcome of my estate planning. But I can assure you that these plans have given me an enormous amount of satisfaction, knowing that the financial results of my lifetime of work will continue to benefit my children, my grandchildren, and the world I love for many, many years after I am gone.

Appendix

Further Resources

This book and the accompanying web site contain everything you need to create a great retirement. But serious students of investing will want to dig further. Here are some suggestions.

ONLINE RESOURCES

These days, most serious investors use their computers for research, reading, monitoring their portfolios, and sometimes trading. Tens of thousands of investor-oriented web sites compete for your attention. Many of them also compete for your mind and your money, often without deserving either.

When I'm on the Web, here are my favorite investment-related sites:

Analyzenow.com is a great site for any serious amateur or professional financial planner. Its creator, former Boeing Aerospace Company President Henry (Bud) Hebeler, has focused his retirement on helping people understand the realities of saving for retirement, as opposed to the fantasies to which many people cling. Casual visitors may find some of his financial planning tools to be conservative and daunting. But they are extremely thorough and reliable, as you would expect from a former aeronautical engineer.

DFAUS.com is the home page for Dimensional Fund Advisors. Here you'll find out more about this firm's investment philosophy along with a large library of academic articles on passive asset class investing. The site also contains several informative videos. Serious investors may find it worthwhile to bookmark the investment glossary on this site.

Morningstar.com offers a huge amount of data and many useful articles covering hundreds of mutual funds. You can learn a great deal by using the site's portfolio analysis tools. Especially useful is the Instant X-Ray tool, which lets you see your portfolio's asset allocation at a glance. I don't think Morningstar's Star ratings for funds and stocks are very useful, but this site's data makes it a must-see for fund research.

AAII.com, the site of the American Association of Individual Investors, offers an extensive article library and numerous handy calculators. This organization does a wonderful job of educating investors about retirement and helping them deal with issues ranging from cash flow to beneficiary designations of retirement accounts.

Vanguard.com has good online calculators for addressing such issues as how much you should save for retirement, whether you can afford to retire, what kind of IRA is best for you, and whether you should roll over your company stock or convert your IRA to a Roth. Others tackle questions regarding saving for college.

TRowePrice.com has a wide range of excellent tools for planning retirement, college funding, estate planning, and dealing with taxes. I'm a fan of this company's moderate-to-conservative approach to investing.

FundAdvice.com contains hundreds of articles that I and members of my staff have written over the years. Here's where you'll always find my latest writing as well as dates of upcoming free workshops and other things my company offers. Along with suggested portfolios and a few dozen calculators, you'll find a unique tool: Explode Loads! Use it to find a good no-load alternative to any load fund you may own or be considering.

CBSMarketwatch.com is one of the most popular financial web sites. You'll find a wide variety of top-notch authors and advisors with many different points of view and topic areas including investment planning, tax planning, and personal finance issues.

BOOKS

I keep these titles handy for reference, and I often recommend them to investors.

The Successful Investor Today by Larry Swedroe does a wonderful job of explaining why investing is challenging—and how to overcome the biggest challenges. Larry is a staunch supporter of using index funds to invest in the asset classes that are most likely to produce fine long-term returns. He also does a fine job of showing how—and why—investors should minimize their expenses.

The Four Pillars of Investing by William Bernstein lays out investment history, both pleasant and unpleasant, to illustrate risks and rewards. It's written well enough that it's worth buying for high school and college students who want to learn how to manage money.

Fooled by Randomness by Nassim Taleb nails a topic every investor must understand in order to be successful. The subtitle says it well: "The Hidden Role of Chance in Life and in the Markets." Unfortunately, many lucky investors think they succeed by being smart. This leads them to try to repeat whatever they believe caused their success, often with disappointing results. To the extent that this book helps investors adopt a little more humble attitude, it will make it easier for them to do the things that stack the odds in their favor.

Why Smart People Make Dumb Mistakes by Gary Belsky and Thomas Gilovich is a great introduction to the field of behaviorial economics, the study of why we make the decisions that we do. Most people operate on "rules of thumb," which too often dictate decisions that should be made by applying logic and reason to specific circumstances. You'll learn how your actions are probably being undermined by aversion to losses, resistance to change, and overconfidence, among other things. This would be an excellent book to give any young person.

Winning the Loser's Game by Charles Ellis puts forth his contributions to modern portfolio theory in an easy-to-read form. Read this book before you bet much money on the premise that you can beat the market.

The Coffeehouse Investor by Bill Schultheis advocates a relatively simple approach to managing money that leaves time and energy (and money) for nonfinancial aspects of life like mountain climbing, golf, and cooking (to mention three of the author's personal passions).

Common Sense on Mutual Funds by John Bogle makes a strong case for low-cost index funds, which should be no surprise from the founder of the Vanguard Group. Bogle also gives an autobiographical glimpse at his life in the fund industry.

The Lazy Person's Guide to Investing by Paul Farrell may give new hope to "financially challenged" procrastinators who want easy approaches to an admittedly difficult subject area. It's better as a first investing book for young people, to spark their interest in the topic and show them lots of possibilities, than as an ultimate guide for retirees or those nearing retirement.

COLUMNISTS

I don't agree with everything by these writers, but they are always worth my time. I think they'll be worth yours, too:

Jonathan Clements of the *Wall Street Journal*

Jason Zweig, senior writer for *Money* magazine

Humberto Cruz, syndicated in multiple newspapers

Charles Jaffe at *CBSMarketwatch.com* and syndicated in multiple newspapers

Mark Hulbert at CBSMarketwatch and in the *New York Times*

Paul Farrell at CBSMarketwatch

Index